1

IELTS
VOCABULARY
MASTERCLASS
8.5

+ IELTS LISTENING & READING DICTIONARY

BOOK 3

Dominate Proficiency Level Vocabulary for IELTS Listening, Reading, Writing & Speaking: (IELTS Vocabulary BOOK 3©)

MARC ROCHE

IELTS VOCABULARY MASTERCLASS 8.5 ©

BOOK 3

+ IELTS LISTENING & READING DICTIONARY

DOMINATE PROFICIENCY LEVEL VOCABULARY FOR IELTS LISTENING, READING, WRITING & SPEAKING

IELTS VOCABULARY BOOK 3 ©

MARC ROCHE

8.5

"You can't build up a vocabulary if you never meet any new words. And to meet them you must read."

- Rudolf Flesch

Disclaimer

Although the author and publisher have made every effort to ensure that the information in this book was correct at press time, the author and publisher do not assume and hereby disclaim any liability to any party for any loss, damage, or disruption caused by errors or omissions, whether such errors or omissions result from negligence, accident, or any other cause.

Topics covered in this book-

IELTS vocabulary, IELTS listening, IELTS grammar, IELTS speaking, IELTS writing, IELTS reading, IELTS academic, IELTS General Training

Table of Contents

GET MARC ROCHE'S STARTER LIBRARY FOR FREE

Sign up for exclusive content via email and get an introductory book and lots more, all for free.

Details can be found at the end of the book.

DEDICATION

For my beautiful son, who brightens my day with his smile, his questions and his mischief.

For my parents, who have always been there.

For Maddi, for being such a wonderful mother to my son.

EPIGRAPH

Your inability to see other possibilities and your lack of vocabulary are your brain's limits, not the universe's.

- Scott Adams

One forgets words as one forgets names. One's vocabulary needs constant fertilizing or it will die.

- Evelyn Waugh

How to Use This Book

IELTS Vocabulary Masterclass 8.5 © BOOK 3 + IELTS Listening & Reading Dictionary - Dominate Proficiency Level Vocabulary for IELTS Listening, Reading, Writing & Speaking (IELTS VOCABULARY BOOK 3 ©)

The Masterclass to 8.5 is simple:

This book is not designed to be an exhaustive list of words, but instead, a focused and easy-access guide for exam preparation + an IELTS Listening & Reading Mini-Dictionary. Review any sections that you feel you need to and use them as a starting point for further research and practice.

1. Read the definitions and write down an example sentence for each vocabulary item.

2. At the end of each topic chapter, you'll find an exercise to review your understanding of the vocabulary. The examples in the exercises are fragments from IELTS Speaking, IELTS Writing, IELTS Listening and IELTS Reading style questions and answers. After reading the definitions, complete the example sentences, using the words in the chapter.

3. Check your answers.

4. Check your original sentence again and see if it needs corrections.

5. Make clean *Notes / write a definition in your own words and an example sentence in your *Notes.

6. Re-read your *Notes twice per day and practise saying the sentences.

7. There is an IELTS Listening and Reading Mini-Dictionary for quick reference.

8. This is a perfect addition to IELTS Vocabulary 8.5 Masterclass Book 1 & Book 2, but also to the book IELTS Speaking 8.5 Masterclass and IELTS Writing 8.5 Masterclass. Practice answering the speaking activities (speaking cards and exam questions) at the back of the book IELTS Speaking 8.5 Masterclass in front of a mirror or with a partner if possible. When you do this, apply time limits to make it more like the real exam and use language from this book to instantly improve your speaking score!

9. Use the "Blank Notes Section" at the end of this workbook to add your own notes and record your progress.

ABOUT THE AUTHOR

Marc is originally from Manchester and currently lives in Spain. He is a writer, teacher, trainer, and entrepreneur. He has collaborated with organizations such as the British Council, the Royal Melbourne Institute of Technology and University of Technology Sydney among others. Marc has also worked with multinationals such as Nike, GlaxoSmithKline or Bolsas y Mercados.

Learn more about Marc at amazon.com/author/marcroche

OTHER BOOKS BY MARC ROCHE

IELTS Vocabulary Masterclass 8.5 (BOOK 1)

IELTS Vocabulary Masterclass 8.5 (BOOK 2)

IELTS Speaking 8.5 Masterclass

IELTS Writing Masterclass 8.5

Grammar for IELTS 8.5 (Book 1)

IELTS VOCABULARY FOR 8.5: PROFICIENCY VOCABULARY FOR READING, LISTENING, SPEAKING & WRITING SKILLS

TOPIC 1. PEOPLE

Acquaintance= (n) when you know someone well enough to say hello and talk to them when you see them, but they're not a friend.

Sibling = brother or sister

Characteristic = typical

Resemble = when something looks similar to something else, it resembles that thing.

Reliable = something or someone that can be trusted for functional things (something or someone you can rely on).

*Note: the opposite is 'unreliable'

Bond = means a close link or to form a close link if we use it as a verb

Conscious = when your conscious of something it means you're aware of something.

Inherent = a natural part of something is inherent to that thing.

Self-esteem = the level confidence or belief you have in your own abilities and positive qualities.

*Note: Self-esteem is often described as 'high' or 'low'.

Stereotypical = something that fits into the typical ideas about the way it should be.
Tendency = something that happens repeatedly. Trend.
Gender = the sex of a person.
Lifetime = the period of time that something exists or that a person or an animal lives.
Sympathise = when you sympathise with someone it means that you understand their position and situation. It's similar to having empathy.
Hardwired = instinctive behaviour
Habitually = usually

Exercise

Choose a word or phrase from the definitions above and write it in the correct gap below.

- **If there is more than one possible answer, choose the best option for the sentence.**

- **You might need to use the same word or phrase more than once in some cases.**

- **You may need to adapt the form of the word to fit into the sentence. For example, you might need to change a verb to third person singular to ensure subject-verb agreement like *bond-bonds*.**

1. Certain types of bird only live in one place in their entire
   .... *Lifetime*

2. I really ......*bond*...... with all the people who lost their jobs, because nobody wants to be in that situation. I think the government can do more to help them at the moment by doing X, Y and Z for example.

3. I'm ...conscious. that I will need to work very hard to become a doctor, but it's my dream and I'm wiling to make the sacrifice.

4. Getting into a car accident is one of the ...characteristic dangers of driving, so it's very important that drivers pay full attention on the road so we can minimise the risk.

5. White sharks do not ...habitually... attack humans, unless they confuse them with seals. However, they have a really bad reputation, and I think this has contributed to a lot of shark deaths over the years, as they've been actively hunted in many parts of the world.

6. Studies suggest that people with higher ...self-esteem... are more likely to be successful in their careers.

7. I want to study accounting, but I don't think I'm the ...stereotypical... accountant. The stereotypical accountant is a very organised and methodical person who enjoys siting at a desk crunching numbers (making calculations).

8. There is a ...tendency.... nowadays to socialise through technology. I think it has some very clear benefits, but it

needs to be used in moderation. The benefits are X, Y and Z. However, the dangers are A, B and C.

9. I think our desire to improve and grow is ...inherented into us as humans, but it needs to be stimulated. This is why I strongly believe that we need to promote real-world, practical education. If people see that they can learn real-world skills, it will encourage them to keep learning.

10. In my opinion, ...gender... is sadly still and issue we need to tackle in today's workplace. There are still great disparities between male and female employees in terms of wages and opportunities.

11. I don't know her very well, she's not really a friend, she's more of an ...acquaintance

12. The shop offers a discount for....siblings. who sign up for store cards.

13. Adding soy sauce while you're cooking the vegetables gives the dish its ...resemble. Vietnamese flavour.

14. Porche's new 2020 car model ...resemble...... the old 1970s models.

15. It's important for me that my friends are ...reliable... I don't like people who are late or who cancel plans at the last minute.

16. My car is very ...reliable....., it has never broken down.

17. I'm very close to my family, we have a very strong .... bond

18. It's important for people to *sympathise* .... if they work together closely. It's easier to do this in small offices rather than big offices. This is why I prefer working for small companies, as they tend to have a smaller, friendlier environment.

TOPIC 2. HEALTH & MEDICINE

Allergic = when you have a negative physical reaction to a substance.

Harmful = not safe, bad for a person or bad for something.

Appetite/hunger = your desire for something (usually food).

*Note: 'crave' means when you really want something. A strong desire for something.

Lifestyle = the way someone lives their life. Your lifestyle can be active, sedentary, sociable, etc...

Ingredients = the components of a specific medicine, drink, food or dish.

Nutritious = full of vitamins, fat, protein, carbohydrates or other essential components for good health.

Suffer = feel discomfort or pain. It can also be used to describe when something negative happens to you or when you have a negative health condition.

Sedentary = the opposite of active. This is often used to describe jobs, activities and lifestyle.
Psychological = related to psychology or the mind.
Beneficial = good, positive or helpful.
Detrimental = bad or negative. Not helpful
Intake = consumption/the amount you eat or drink.
Eradicate = get rid or something (exterminate)
Well-being = your well-being is your level of comfort, health and happiness.
Severity = the seriousness of something.
Preventive = actions that aim to prevent or stop something

Additives = the chemicals that are added to food and drink to stop it from rotting or to enhance favour.

Preservatives = the chemicals that are added to food and drink to keep it fresh for longer.

Administer= to give a patient a medicine or medical treatment.

Admit = to officially allow someone to stay in hospital for medical care.

Agony = intense physical pain or emotional suffering.

Antidote = a drug that stops the negative effects of a poison.

Consultant = an experienced doctor in a hospital who specialises in a specific area of medicine.

Diagnosis = an official conclusion about a patient's condition, given by a doctor.
Inoculate = to use a vaccine protect people against a disease (to vaccinate).
Nursing home (Care home) = a place where the elderly live when they are not able to look after themselves due to their age or due to an illness.

Exercise

Choose a word or phrase from the definitions above and write it in the correct gap below.

- If there is more than one possible answer, choose the best option for the sentence.

- You might need to use the same word or phrase more than once in some cases.

- You may need to adapt the form of the word to fit into the sentence. For example, you might need to change a verb to third person singular to ensure subject-verb agreement like *bond-bonds*.

1. I don't think I could ever work in an office, as I don't think I'd like that .... I'm an active person who enjoys doing things outdoors and moving around a lot and staying in one place indoors for 8-12 hours a day every day is my idea of hell!

    sedentary = inactive

2. My uncle was ...._suffered_.... with Crohn's disease several years ago, but he still works full-time and hasn't let it stop him from pursuing most of his hobbies.

3. He works as a cardiology .... at a children's hospital in the city centre. His work is very demanding but he's passionate about it. *Consultant*

4. A funny story happened to me on my last birthday. I took my dog to get .... against rabies and someone had brought an abandoned dog into the vet's to try and help it. Long story short, I ended up adopting another dog! *administer* *inoculated*

5. If you get bitten by a poisonous snake, it's important to go to hospital so they can give you an .... *inoculate*

6. There has been a lot of controversy surrounding the level of care in some .... *nursing homes*

7. When I broke my leg I was in ...., so I rang my friend and she took me to hospital. *agony*

8. The more people are .... into hospitals, the higher the demand on medical staff and other resources. *admitted*

9. The drug is .... orally, twice a day. *intaken*

10. It's better for your health of you avoid eating too many foods
    that contain .... *Preservatives*

    additives

11. It was .... when my team lost the championship in the
    last 3 seconds of the game! (This is an exaggeration, but very
    common)

    detrimental

12. Having your heart broken is .... *detrimental*

13. My favourite dish is peperoni pizza. The .... are pizza
    dough, cheese, tomato, peperoni, olive oil and chilly.

    Ingredients

14. Our .... is more important than money. We need
    to focus on this so that we can eradicate this problem.

    Well- being

15. It's important to monitor your daily .... of trans fats.

    additives

16. Too much sugar can be extremely .... to your
    health.

    Preventive   *harmful*

17. .... medicine is often more effective than treatment.
    (It aims to stop diseases before they develop)

18. We underestimated the .... of the situation.

server (crossed out)

severity

19. The government has put .... measures in place so that businesses can recover as quickly as possible.

beneficial

20. We need to .... the problem now or it will cause more damage in the future.

eradicate

allergic

21. I think junk food increases your ...., as it has very little substance. It doesn't fill you for long and makes you crave more.

22. The .... impact of what has happened has been enormous. It has changed the way we live and the way we view the world.

lifestyle

23. I need to exercise more because I have a very .... job, where I spend most of the day sitting down at a desk.

sedentary

24. Avocados are very ...., they are packed with iron, vitamins and healthy fat.

nutritious

25. I .... quite a lot during the lockdown, as I couldn't visit my family.

suffered

26. Jack .... a car accident when he was younger, and it changed his life. He is now extremely successful and responsible.

ad *suffered*

27. People who .... from rare genetic disorders need more guidance from doctors.

suffer

28. It would be .... if we could have more *beneficial* telecommuting from now on, as it reduces potential risks and reduces damage to the environment. It is also cheaper for many companies, so everyone would benefit from this type of change.

29. The pandemic has been very .... to businesses all over the world.

~~harmful~~ detrimental

harmful

30. Smoking is very .... not just to the person smoking, but also to the people around. This is why we need to make it illegal in my opinion.

31. I'm .... to nuts, so I need to be very careful when I
    eat out in restaurants.

    allergic

32. I believe that the government needs to introduce tighter
    restrictions to regulate the .... in natural remedies,
    as they are often potentially dangerous.

    ingredients

Topic 3. Social & Leisure

Conform = to follow social rules.

Cooperate = when people work well together

Mindset (frame of mind) = the way you think. Your mental attitude at a particular point in your life or in a particular situation.

Minority = a small percentage of a group or population.

Shun = to reject

We can't …….. our responsibility as citizens. We have to be sensible and responsible to prevent dangerous situations like this from happening again.

Conventional = the usual, normal or traditional way of doing something or thinking. 'Conventional wisdom' is an expression, meaning: what most people believe to be true, or what most experts accept as the truth.

normal way

Interaction = communication between people (written, spoken or through sign language for example).

Pressure = stress or expectations.

Conduct = This can be used as verb and as a noun meaning behaviour-behave. When used as a verb to mean 'behave', it is reflexive, meaning it goes with myself, yourself, himself, herself etc..

Pronunciation *Note: the stress is on the first syllable when it's used as a noun and on the second syllable when used as a verb.

Mainstream = common likes or ideas. Popular

Appropriate = acceptable or suitable for a particular situation.

Multicultural = something that has several different cultures. It can be a team, a department, a city, a country etc..

Absorbing = something that entertains you so much, that you forget about everything else.

Exhilarating = something that makes you feel full of energy and excitement. Thrilling.

Indulge = to do something that you like (like a reward).

Pursue = to follow an activity in order to reach a goal. Think of chasing your dreams.
Tedious = not exciting. Focusing on highly specific but boring things (in the speaker's opinion).
Trivial = unimportant
Unwind = to begin the process of relaxation after stress or hard work
Foster = to protect something and encourage it to grow (an idea, an attitude, a feeling, an action or a result).

Exercise

Choose a word or phrase from the definitions above and write it in the correct gap below.

- If there is more than one possible answer, choose the best option for the sentence.

- You might need to use the same word or phrase more than once in some cases.

- You may need to adapt the form of the word to fit into the sentence. For example, you might need to change a verb to third person singular to ensure subject-verb agreement like *bond-bonds.*

1. I decided to .... myself and had a weekend in New York. *unwind*

2. I usually like to .... *indulge* by doing some exercise and meeting up with some friends at the weekend. We have a few drinks and go out for dinner or we watch a film. I also like to unwind at the end of the day by reading and listening to some music. It really helps to clear my mind.

3. Lots of decisions that we think are really important when we're younger seem .... when we get older.

trivial

4. I found paragliding .... I was hooked from the first time I tried it.

5. I really want to study and work in London, because it's *multicultural* such a .... place. I love walking down the street and seeing all the different people from all over the world, or, going to the markets and chatting to the locals.

6. The film was ...., I couldn't take my eyes off the *exhilarating* screen (it had us glued to the screen). From the plot, to the characters and setting, I thought it was all incredible.

7. I want to ..*pursue*... a career in engineering.

8. I find numbers and Maths quite ..*tedious*.., I'm much more interested in biology.

9. The government has introduced policies that .... fair competition among companies.

conform

10. Turning up to a formal office job interview in shorts is not .... obviously, so they rejected him. This made him re-examine his life.

11. I live quite a .... life during the week. I live in a small apartment in the city centre and I work and study most days. However, at the weekends, I work as a magician at private events around the country!

12. According to .... wisdom in Hollywood, films can't make a profit unless they have big name actors and actresses and large budgets. I really like films that defy those odds.

   *Note: 'defy the odds' means to succeed despite what people believe or despite low probability of success.

13. There is a .... of people who agree with this political party's policies, but the majority of the population are against them.

14. People judge you based on how you .... yourself more than on how you dress, even though the way you dress is also a big factor.

15. There is too much .... on young people today. People expect us to have everything figured out by the time we're 18, but that doesn't usually happen. I know people who are in the 40s and are still figuring their life out and deciding what they want to do!

16. Social media and the internet in general have changed our ....

17. My favourite band, the Snake Patrol, were not very well known when they started, but then they released that song 'Slither in the Wind' and they became .... Suddenly, everyone was listening to them.

18. It's important to .... with your class mates because it makes projects easier and it helps you learn faster, as you can learn from each other.

19. I really admire my father because he refuses to .... to what society dictates. When people told him that he should go to university and study law, he refused. Instead, he started his own business when he had no money and he made it successful through hard work and effort.

20. When you train for an important football match, it's important to keep a positive .... and constantly try to make small improvements. It's important to view your mistakes as lessons rather than failures.

TOPIC 4. EDUCATION

Theoretical = coming from theories, not practice. It's another way of saying that something has not been proven in the real world. Theoretical is also used as an adjective to describe something that focuses on abstract concepts rather than practicing a skill.

Acquire = to buy with money, get by chance or gain through effort.

Please *Note: It's quite a formal verb, so it is often used in every day conversation with a little bit of irony. It's used as a colourful alternative to 'buy', 'get', or 'gain' in informal conversations. In formal conversations, it's often used in interviews (to talk about skills or experience you have acquired) or speaking exams like IELTS.

Valid = acceptable or reasonable

Determine = find out, discover or decide after doing research

Establish = prove or consolidate
Significant = meaningful or important
Miscalculation = a mistake, using bad judgment or making an error in a calculation.
Methodical = being organised or careful and patient when you do something.
Cram = to overload the brain by trying to learn a lot in a short period of time.
Compulsory = obligatory, something you HAVE to do

Exercise

Choose a word or phrase from the definitions above and write it in the correct gap below.

- **If there is more than one possible answer, choose the best option for the sentence.**

- **You might need to use the same word or phrase more than once in some cases.**

- **You may need to adapt the form of the word to fit into the sentence. For example, you might need to change a verb to third person singular to ensure subject-verb agreement like *bond-bonds*.**

1. First, I have to .... whether I should study a Masters' degree or whether I should try to gain more industry experience.

2. Talk about a .... day in your life.
   You should say:
   When it was.
   What happened.
   Why it was .... and how it made you feel.

Answer: *Ok, the most meaningful/important day I can remember is blah blah blah*

3. They should .... where the virus came from first, and then establish ways to prevent this from happening again in the future.

4. I always say that I'm going to be really organised for my tests, but I always end up .... it all in at the last minute!

5. I think that choosing this venue for the event was a .... on my part, as they were completely unprepared and didn-t offer any of the services they advertised. I really should have checked their reviews first.

6. I think that in order to be as successful as possible at university, you need to be .... by always keeping an organised *Notebook and by always categorising your *Notes into sections.

7. I believe that it should be .... to have some sort of practical training as part of your degree. I think

that getting industry experience is vital in today's job market.

> *Note: 'Industry experience' is a term which literally means experience of working in the sector where you want to be employed. (It can be work experience placements or full-time jobs you've had in the past)

8. I recently .... a new watch, which I have completely fallen in love with!

9. The idea that time-travel is possible is purely .... We don't actually know because it is currently impossible to test the theory.

10. You make a .... point. (This means: 'What you're saying is fair').

11. I think it's important to have a .... component in a Business course so you can understand certain concepts, but you also need a practical component, so you can learn how to implement those concepts in the real world.

12. Talk about something you've .... recently.

> *You should mention:*

What It is
When you .... it.
How you .... it and why it's important to you.

*Note: In this example you could talk about something you have bought or a skill you have obtained through your efforts.

TOPIC 5: ADVERTISING

Persuade = convince someone of something
Unavoidable = certain to happen
Effective = when something achieves its purpose
Ploy = trick
Intrusive = invasive
Hype-up = a phrasal verb meaning to exaggerate for a commercial or public relations interest **Hype=** we also use 'hype' as a noun meaning exaggeration (usually for commercial reasons)
Endorse = officially recommend a product or a company
Gullible = too trusting or easy to trick
Prominent = noticeable or extraordinary

Entice = tempt by offering something
Bombard = continuously direct something towards someone
Inescapable = something you can't avoid.

Exercise

Choose a word or phrase from the definitions above and write it in the correct gap below.

- If there is more than one possible answer, choose the best option for the sentence.

- You might need to use the same word or phrase more than once in some cases.

- You may need to adapt the form of the word to fit into the sentence. For example, you might need to change a verb to third person singular to ensure subject-verb agreement like *bond-bonds.*

1. If you allow advertisers to promote gambling, people will gamble more. It's ....

2. We are constantly .... with adverts every day on TV, online, on the radio, in newspapers and even on the street. It seems like everywhere we look there's an advert.

3. I think we are all quite ………………… as consumers. We often believe companies just because they advertise on TV.

4. It seems like everywhere we look there's an advert, it's ………………….

5. Fast food companies ………… us with adverts of delicious looking food, but when you actually try it, it's often disappointing.

6. ……………… advertising sells products and creates brand awareness.

7. A ………………… marketing guru argues that all publicity, whether it's positive or negative, is actually good for a company.

8. Shops use special discounts as a marketing ……………… to encourage people to go into their shops and buy other products. People go into the shop for the discount and end up buying products that are not on discount.

9. I find .... advertising like internet popups and cookies really annoying.

10. The role of advertising is to .... customers to buy products they don't necessarily need.

11. It's important to ignore the .... when you're trying to choose a good restaurant.

12. Most companies .... their products to sell more.

13. Nike are .... by famous professional footballers all over the world.

Topic 6: Travel & places

Memorable = something special or unforgettable
Custom = a local tradition or habit
Remote = isolated or far away
Spectacular = stunning, amazing or very impressive
Landscape = large natural area of land
Basic = simple, not complicated or luxurious. (Often used to describe accommodation)
Barren = without vegetation
Wander = walk without a specific destination

Exercise

Choose a word or phrase from the definitions above and write it in the correct gap below.

- If there is more than one possible answer, choose the best option for the sentence.

- You might need to use the same word or phrase more than once in some cases.

- You may need to adapt the form of the word to fit into the sentence. For example, you might need to change a verb to third person singular to ensure subject-verb agreement like *bond-bonds.*

1. It's a .... to eat cheese and cold-cuts in Mediterranean countries such as Spain and Italy.

2. On our first day in Berlin, we .... around the city and explored different markets and bars around the centre.

3. The landscape is quite ...., but it's stunningly beautiful. The sunsets in particular are amazing.

4. During our trip to Thailand, we visited a .... island just off the coast of Phuket. It was spectacular.

5. When I visited Bangkok, I ate the most .... food and the temples were absolutely stunning.

6. The South of Spain has some amazing .... In some areas, you can go skiing in the mornings and then go to the hot beach in the afternoon. It's stunning.

7. Our hotel was really ...., but we only used it as a place to sleep. We spent most of our time outside, exploring the city and going on guided tours. It was an amazing experience.

8. Traveling round America with my family was a .... experience. We managed to visit six states in total and did an amazing road trip down Route 66.

Topic 7: Animals

Endangered = a species of animal or plant that's dying.
Venomous = poisonous
Domesticated = trained to live with humans in houses instead of in the wild.
Thrive = grow strong
Vulnerable = something that can be hurt or that is in danger.
Dwindle = shrink in numbers, become fewer or weaker
Habitat = Natural environment of an animal or plant species.
Survival = continuing to exist
Co-exist = live in the same time or place

Exercise

Choose a word or phrase from the definitions above and write it in the correct gap below.

- If there is more than one possible answer, choose the best option for the sentence.

- You might need to use the same word or phrase more than once in some cases.

- You may need to adapt the form of the word to fit into the sentence. For example, you might need to change a verb to third person singular to ensure subject-verb agreement like *bond-bonds.*

1. We must put stricter systems in place in order to ensure the .... of species such as chimpanzees, mountain gorillas and orangutans.

2. The large human presence in the area has had a negative effect on fish ....

3. Higher penalties could stop smugglers, protect public health and help preserve .... species such as tigers.

4. While many animals are already facing and will continue to face serious problems due to global warming, some species will actually .... on a warming planet.

5. Humans can .... with plants and other animals, we just need to see it as a major priority. I strongly believe that in ten or twenty-years-time it will be too late to reverse the effects of global warming. We must act now; our survival depends on it.

6. The Mountain Gorilla is one of the most critically .... animals on the planet.

7. Scientists recently created the largest botanical dataset ever and discovered that almost 40% of plant species that live on land are potentially .... to global warming. If we don't make radical changes now, we risk losing these species in the next few years. This will be carry disastrous consequences for human beings.

8. I think it's important to remember that not all animals can be or should be .... I honestly believe that people should not be allowed to have pets like snakes, birds or monkeys. It's cruel and potentially dangerous in my opinion.

9. Many people assume that most snakes are poisonous, but of the 3,500 snake species around the world, only 600 are actually ....

Topic 8: Technology and Computers

Virtual = in a computer or simulation, not in the real world
Digital = computerised rather than physical. Often used to refer to information and information products.
Embrace = happily accept
Addictive = when something makes people want more and more
Security (Secure) = Safety (Safe)
Cutting-edge = the newest or most advanced technology, design or method.
Cyberbullying = attacking other people online
Technological = relate to technology
Dated = not relevant or true anymore because things have changed

Domestic appliances = machines we use in our homes

'White-goods', means domestic appliances like washing machines and dishwashers, but doesn't usually include devices like blenders or air fryers for example.

Surpass = Be or do more than. Do something better than or be better than. Be bigger than, higher than, faster than etc.

Upgrade = get a better-quality version of something

Innovative = creative and new

Exercise

Choose a word or phrase from the definitions above and write it in the correct gap below.

- If there is more than one possible answer, choose the best option for the sentence.

- You might need to use the same word or phrase more than once in some cases.

- You may need to adapt the form of the word to fit into the sentence. For example, you might need to change a verb to third person singular to ensure subject-verb agreement like *bond-bonds.*

1. As humans, we continually strive to .... what we can do and what we think is possible. I think it's mind-boggling to think about the technology we might have in 1-200 years, and the things that will be possible in 500 years. It just blows my mind!

   *Note: 'mind-boggling' means 'amazing' or 'incredible'. 'It blows my mind' or it's 'mind blowing' means the same. It's something so amazing or interesting, that it excites you and makes you feel a sense of wonder.

2. Sales of ………… books, or e-books, have been rising steadily for years now.

3. My favourite possession is my new phone. I bought it last week. This particular model contains a …………………… processor which makes it 50% faster than the previous model from the same brand. I also love the design, as it's sleek and robust at the same time.

   *Note: 'Sleek' means smooth or stylish, while 'robust' means strong and durable. In the example you could have also talked about its '……………. design' instead of its processor.

4. …………………… is a huge issue nowadays, because victims cannot escape the bullying.

5. It would be an absolute game-changer if the government could introduce a policy of upgrading ………… technology with cutting-edge energy efficient models, improving performance and energy consumption.

   *Note: a 'game-changer' or 'game-changing', means a radical change (usually positive). Something that would change everything if it was applied in this example.

6. .... form part of a multi-billion-dollar industry. Although many of them are extremely handy, we often end up buying devices we don't need and that don't even make our lives any easier. *Note: 'Handy' means convenient.

7. The .... era has brought many benefits to our lives. In my opinion, it has massively improved human interaction by providing us with more options to connect with people from all over the planet and to keep in touch with family and friends when we're far away. It has allowed us to communicate during times of crisis and it allows us to work together for common goals. None of this was possible (would have been possible) thirty years ago.

8. Some of the most .... inventions in human history have been born out of pure necessity. It's a total cliché, but necessity really is the mother of invention.

    *Note: 'Necessity is the mother of invention' is an expression in English and in several other languages. It means that humans invent things they need. In times of extreme need we think of our most creative ideas in order to survive.

9. I know it's a bit of a cliché, but I still believe that .... reality is the future of entertainment.

10. I think that as a society, we're not paying enough attention to the fact that technology is very .... While it can be extremely beneficial, there are also many potential drawbacks.

    **Note: 'drawbacks' is like saying 'disadvantages'

11. Data .... is a massive issue at the moment, and rightfully so. Companies hold a lot of information about us, and it would be dangerous in the wrong hands.

    *Note: 'and rightfully so', is an informal phrase we use at the end of sentences to state that what we've just mentioned is justified.

    Examples could be:
    Smoking has been banned in public spaces, and rightfully so!

    When they didn't send her the product she'd paid for, she demanded her money back, and rightfully so!

12. Not everyone has .... this new era of reading on your phone or on other electronic devices. Many people still prefer to read books the traditional way.

13. We decided to .... our kitchen, replacing all of our outdated appliances with new cutting-edge ones.

TOPIC 9: FASHION

Shoppers = people who buy from retail stores.
Passing = short. Something that will disappear quickly
Trendy = fashionable
Impulsive = an action carried out without thinking. Or a person who doesn't think before acting.
Consumerism = the behaviour or culture of buying things we don't necessarily need.
Purchase = in the noun form, this means something that has been bought. In the verb form, it means 'buy'.

Exercise

Choose a word or phrase from the definitions above and write it in the correct gap below.

- **If there is more than one possible answer, choose the best option for the sentence.**

- **You might need to use the same word or phrase more than once in some cases.**

- **You may need to adapt the form of the word to fit into the sentence. For example, you might need to change a verb to third person singular to ensure subject-verb agreement like *bond-bonds*.**

1. I believe that some people choose clothes only because they are ...., but I don't think most people do that. I think most people choose the clothes they like within the current trends.

2. The most memorable thing I've ever .... is my car. It gives me independence and freedom, so I can go wherever I want. It allows me to study and work and it allows me to visit my friends and family. Having it has completely changed my life for the better.

3. I really hope responsible fashion isn't a ……………… trend. I hope that the top brands in the industry will take a more active role in the near-future, as more people recognise the importance of being environmentally-conscious.

4. ……………… buying is a habit that I would like to stop! Whenever I go to a shopping centre I always end up buying something. I find it really hard to resist!

5. I think ………………… is mostly negative, because it makes us focus on things that aren't important. Many people put more time and effort into obtaining material possessions than they do into improving themselves as human beings.

6. *Examiner Question:* Why do some people enjoy clothes shopping?

   Candidate Answer: Good question! I think some ………… enjoy the experience of walking around the different shops trying things on. Many people also go with friends or family and make it into a social outing. They go for lunch, or for coffee, or they go to the cinema after shopping.

7. I had to borrow money to ………………… my first car.

TOPIC 10: CITY LIFE

Inadequate = not good enough
Transportation (transport) = the type of vehicle you use to travel
Pedestrian = person walking on the street
Commute = In the noun form, this means your journey to school or work. In the verb for, it means to travel to work or school.
Pavement = the place where pedestrians should walk on the street (not the road).
Slums = very poor-quality housing, often without running water or electricity.
Infrastructure = services and basic structures in an area. Infra- means 'below;' so the infrastructure is the 'basic structure below' a country, an economy, a business or an organisation.
Overpopulated (overpopulation)= when there are too many people in an area.

Outskirts = the edge of a city, town or village.

Isolated = separated from others

Inequality = The opposite of equality. Disparity or imbalance in something. Often used to talk about people's rights or living standards.

Overwhelmed = unable to deal with a situation

Shortage = a lack of something

Affluent = rich / wealthy / prosperous

Run-down = when talking about things it means old and neglected. When talking about humans, 'run-down' means tired-looking or looking slightly ill.

Exercise

Choose a word or phrase from the definitions above and write it in the correct gap below.

- If there is more than one possible answer, choose the best option for the sentence.

- You might need to use the same word or phrase more than once in some cases.

- You may need to adapt the form of the word to fit into the sentence. For example, you might need to change a verb to third person singular to ensure subject-verb agreement like *bond-bonds.*

1. I found Amsterdam to be very ....-friendly, as there are very few cars, and the bikes there are quite respectful of the people walking around.

2. Water .... cause major problems in some areas of the country.

3. Public .... in my home town is great. There are buses every fifteen minutes and train lines every twenty

minutes. You can be anywhere in town within twenty minutes.

4. One third of the people in the city live in .... They don't have electricity or running water.

5. More funding is required to boost the crumbling ....of the country's production plants.

   *Notes:
   Funding = Money
   Required = Needed
   Boost = Improve or revitalise
   Crumbling = decaying or run-down

6. I have to .... for one hour every day to get to class!

7. The .... are quite run-down in my neighbourhood, but the council don't have enough money to fix them.

8. Half of the city's population live in .... housing. The conditions are quite bad for these people, as most of them don't have running water.

9. I grew up on the .... of the city, but I moved closer to the centre when I started working. The commute was just too long to do every day!

10. The .... in urban areas has led to an increase in pollution and inadequate housing among other issues. This is something that needs to be addressed sooner rather than later.

   *Note: 'sooner rather than later' is an expression to emphasise that something needs to be done now not in the future.

11. John Milton proposed a new system designed to remove .... in health care but it was rejected by his own political party.

12. The healthcare system was initially ....by the sheer number of infections. They couldn't handle it.

   *Note: the word 'sheer' is used to express that the only thing that affected the situation was the thing you're talking about. In the example, 'the number of infections', the number of infections was the only or main cause of the problem.

13. When I travelled round Mexico, I visited an ....
    community in the middle of the desert. It was really
    interesting. Most of the people there had never seen a
    foreigner before, so they were really curious. They were
    so welcoming and kind that I actually felt a bit sad when I
    had to leave.

14. Some parts of my city are quite ...., but the
    centre is very nice to walk around and has many hidden
    gems.

15. I really admire my uncle Bob, because he grew up in a
    very deprived area, but he managed to set up several
    businesses and he now lives in one of the most
    .... areas in town. I admire his drive and
    ambition, as well as his creativity.

    *Notes:
    Deprived= poor
    Grow up= when you're raised in a certain place
    Set up = start businesses or projects
    Drive= Determination (refusing to be defeated)

TOPIC 11: ENVIRONMENT

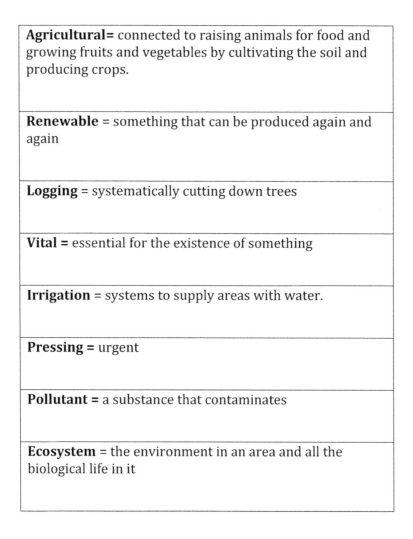

Agricultural= connected to raising animals for food and growing fruits and vegetables by cultivating the soil and producing crops.

Renewable = something that can be produced again and again

Logging = systematically cutting down trees

Vital = essential for the existence of something

Irrigation = systems to supply areas with water.

Pressing = urgent

Pollutant = a substance that contaminates

Ecosystem = the environment in an area and all the biological life in it

Unprecedented = something that has never happened before

Safeguard = protect against something

Exercise

Choose a word or phrase from the definitions above and write it in the correct gap below.

- If there is more than one possible answer, choose the best option for the sentence.

- You might need to use the same word or phrase more than once in some cases.

- You may need to adapt the form of the word to fit into the sentence. For example, you might need to change a verb to third person singular to ensure subject-verb agreement like *bond-bonds.*

1. Trees are .... for the environment.

2. We must .... the environment against the destruction of habitats and the over-exploitation of natural resources such as fresh water and fisheries among other issues.

3. The most dangerous gaseous air .... released into the air in urban areas are Sulphur dioxide, nitrogen dioxide, and carbon monoxide;

4. I grew up in an .... community so farming was still in my blood.

5. .... is a major issue in many forests and jungles all over the world. As more trees are chopped down, these natural areas are shrinking more and more.

6. Trees are .... natural resources, but they should be treated with extreme care.

7. Lack of investment in new methods may result in deterioration of the .... system in the area and a subsequent decline of the local economy.

   *Notes:

   Deterioration= decay. When something breaks down and dissolves

   Subsequent= eventual. When something happens as a result of something else.

8. There is a .... need for housing in the area.

9. Half of these trees could be gone within five years, threatening jobs and ………………

10. Governments were not sure how to deal with the situation because it was ……………. in 21st-century life.

Topic 12: Media

Tabloid = newspapers that are not as serious and impartial
Impartial = neutral
Biased = not neutral or impartial
Escapism = a noun to describe when you use something to forget about normal life and escape your problems.
Medium = singular noun for media. Media is plural (most people don't realise).
Well informed = having enough high-quality information to understand and make good decisions
Scrutinise = examine or analyse carefully
Censor = to remove parts of what is said or published in the media or in any form of communication because you don't want someone to see, read or hear that information.

Manipulate = to control someone or something indirectly (has a negative connotation)
Spotlight = public attention / publicity / limelight / being in the public eye
Imply = to suggest something without saying it directly

Exercise

Choose a word or phrase from the definitions above and write it in the correct gap below.

- If there is more than one possible answer, choose the best option for the sentence.

- You might need to use the same word or phrase more than once in some cases.

- You may need to adapt the form of the word to fit into the sentence. For example, you might need to change a verb to third person singular to ensure subject-verb agreement like *bond-bonds*.

1. The President's blunders gave the .... press great satisfaction.

2. The media .... that there had been a cover-up. They never said it directly, but it was the logical conclusion from the way they reported the whole story.

   *Note: a 'cover-up' is when governments or businesses try to stop the public from finding out about something serious.

3. It's important to .... politicians to ensure that they are honest and trustworthy.

4. Interactive series and films open up the .... of video platforms to the participation of viewers.

5. For many people watching fantasy series and films on Netflix or on TV is a form of ....

6. I think the government and the media .... us in many ways. They report the news the way they want us to see it.

7. The tabloid press gave a very .... account of the situation.

   *Note: the word 'account' means 'report' in this context.

8. I completely disagree with any initiatives which aim to .... the Internet in any way, shape or form.

   *Note: 'in any way, shape or form' means 'in any way', but adds extra emphasis.

9. A judge has to be fair and ...., or the law loses all meaning.

    *Note: when something 'loses all meaning', we mean that it loses its purpose or value in some way.

10. Consumers need to be .... about the side effects of so-called natural remedies.

    *Note: 'So-called' is used to communicate to the listener that you believe a word that is used to describe someone or something is wrong in some way.

11. I think many celebrities struggle with living their lives in the .... It must be very hard to have every part of your life scrutinised by strangers.

FULL NOTES SECTION WITH ANSWERS

TOPIC 1. PEOPLE

Acquaintance= (n) when you know someone well enough to say hello and talk to them when you see them, but they're not a friend.

For example: I don't know her very well, she's not really a friend, she's more of an acquaintance.

Sibling = brother or sister

For example: The shop offers a discount for siblings who sign up for store cards.

Characteristic = typical

For example: Adding soy sauce while you're cooking the vegetables gives the dish its characteristic Vietnamese flavour.

Resemble = when something looks similar to something else, it resembles that thing.

For example: Porche's new 2020 car model resembles the old 1970s models.

Reliable = something or someone that can be trusted for functional things (something or someone you can rely on).

For example:

It's important for me that my friends are reliable, I don't

like people who are late or who cancel plans at the last minute.

My car is very reliable, it has never broken down.

*Note: the opposite is 'unreliable'

Bond = means a close link or to form a close link if we use it as a verb

For example (noun): I'm very close to my family, we have a very strong bond.

For example (verb): It's important for people to bond if they work together closely. It's easier to do this in small offices rather than big offices. This is why I prefer working for small companies, as they tend to have a smaller, friendlier environment.

Conscious = when your conscious of something it means you're aware of something.

For example: I'm conscious that I will need to work very hard to become a doctor, but it's my dream and I'm wiling to make the sacrifice.

Inherent = a natural part of something is inherent to that thing.

For example: Getting into a car accident is one of the inherent dangers of driving, so it's very important that drivers pay full attention on the road so we can minimise the risk.

Self-esteem = the level confidence or belief you have in your own abilities and positive qualities.

For example: Studies suggest that people with higher self-esteem are more likely to be successful in their careers.

*Note: Self-esteem is often described as 'high' or 'low'.

Stereotypical = something that fits into the typical ideas about the way it should be.

For example: I want to study accounting, but I don't think I'm the stereotypical accountant. The stereotypical accountant is a very organised and methodical person who enjoys siting at a desk crunching numbers (making calculations).

Tendency = something that happens repeatedly. Trend.

For example: There is a tendency nowadays to socialise through technology. I think it has some very clear benefits, but it needs to be used in moderation. The benefits are X, Y and Z. However, the dangers are A, B and C.

Gender = the sex of a person.

For example: In my opinion, gender is sadly still and issue we need to tackle in today's workplace. There are still great disparities between male and female employees in terms of wages and opportunities.

Lifetime = the period of time that something exists or that a person or an animal lives.

For example: Certain types of bird only live in one place in their entire lifetime.

Sympathise = when you sympathise with someone it means that you understand their position and situation. It's similar to having empathy.

For example: I really sympathise with all the people who lost their jobs, because nobody wants to be in that situation. I think the government can do more to help them at the moment by doing X, Y and Z for example.

Hardwired = instinctive behaviour

For example: I think our desire to improve and grow is hardwired into us as humans, but it needs to be stimulated. This is why I strongly believe that we need to promote real-world, practical education. If people see that they can learn real-world skills, it will encourage them to keep learning.

Habitually = usually

For example: White sharks do not habitually attack humans, unless they confuse them with seals. However, they have a really bad reputation, and I think this has contributed to a lot of shark deaths over the years, as they've been actively hunted in many parts of the world.

Topic 2. Health & Medicine

Allergic = when you have a negative physical reaction to a substance.

For example: I'm allergic to nuts, so I need to be very careful when I eat out in restaurants.

Harmful = not safe, bad for a person or bad for something.

For example: Smoking is very harmful not just to the person smoking, but also to the people around. This is why we need to make it illegal in my opinion.

For example: The pandemic has been very harmful to businesses all over the world.

Appetite/hunger = your desire for something (usually food).

For example: I think junk food increases your appetite, as it has very little substance. It doesn't fill you for long and makes you crave more.

*Note: 'crave' means when you really want something. A strong desire for something.

Lifestyle = the way someone lives their life. Your lifestyle can be active, sedentary, sociable, etc...

For example: I don't think I could ever work in an office, as I don't think I'd like that lifestyle. I'm an active person who enjoys doing things outdoors and moving around a lot, and staying in one place indoors for 8-12 hours a day everyday is my idea of hell!

Ingredients = the components of a specific medicine, drink, food or dish.

For example: I believe that the government needs to introduce tighter restrictions to regulate the ingredients of natural remedies, as they are often potentially dangerous.

For example: My favourite dish is peperoni pizza. The ingredients are pizza dough, cheese, tomato, peperoni, olive oil and chilly.

Nutritious = full of vitamins, fat, protein, carbohydrates or other essential components for good health.

For example: Avocados are very nutritious, they are packed with iron, vitamins and healthy fat.

Suffer = feel discomfort or pain. It can also be used to describe when something negative happens to you or when you have a negative health condition.

For example: I suffered quite a lot during the lockdown, as I couldn't visit my family.

For example: Jack suffered a car accident when he was younger, and it changed his life. He is now extremely successful and responsible.

For example: People who suffer from rare genetic disorders need more guidance from doctors.

Sedentary = the opposite of active. This is often used to describe jobs, activities and lifestyle.

For example: I need to exercise more because I have a very sedentary job, where I spend most of the day sitting down at a desk.

Psychological = related to psychology or the mind.

For example: The psychological impact of what has happened has been enormous. It has changed the way we live and the way we view the world.

Beneficial = good, positive or helpful.

For example: It would be beneficial if we could have more telecommuting from now on, as it reduces potential risks and reduces damage to the environment. It is also cheaper for many companies, so everyone would benefit from this type of change.

Detrimental = bad or negative. Not helpful

For example: Too much sugar can be extremely detrimental to your health.

Intake = the amount you eat or drink.

For example: It's important to monitor your daily intake of trans fats.

Eradicate = get rid or something (exterminate)

For example: We need to eradicate the problem now or it will cause more damage in the future.

Well-being = your well-being is your level of comfort, health and happiness. For example: Our well-being is more important than money. We need to focus on this so that we can eradicate this problem.
Severity = the seriousness of something. For example: We underestimated the severity of the situation.
Preventive = actions that aim to prevent or stop something For example: Preventive medicine is often more effective than treatment. For example: The government has put preventive measures in place so that businesses can recover as quickly as possible.
Additives = the chemicals that are added to food and drink to stop it from rotting or to enhance favour. Preservatives = the chemicals that are added to food and drink to keep it fresh for longer. For example: It's better for your health of you avoid eating too many foods that contain additives / preservatives.
Administer= to give a patient a medicine or medical treatment.

For example: The drug is administered orally, twice a day.

Admit = to officially allow someone to stay in hospital for medical care.

For example: The more people are admitted into hospitals, the higher the demand on medical staff and other resources.

Agony = intense physical pain or emotional suffering.

For example: When I broke my leg I was in agony, so I rang my friend and she took me to hospital.

For example: It was agonising/agony when my team lost the championship in the last 3 seconds of the game! (This is an exaggeration)

For example: Having your heart broken is agony/agonising.

Antidote = a drug that stops the negative effects of a poison.

For example: If you get bitten by a poisonous snake, it's important to go to hospital so they can give you an antidote.

Consultant = an experienced doctor in a hospital who specialises in a specific area of medicine.

For example: He works as a cardiology consultant at a children's hospital in the city centre. His work is very demanding but he's passionate about it.

Diagnosis = an official conclusion about a patient's condition, given by a doctor.

For example: My uncle was diagnosed with Crohn's disease several years ago, but he still works full-time and hasn't let it stop him from pursuing most of his hobbies.

Inoculate = to use a vaccine protect people against a disease (to vaccinate)

For example: A funny story happened to me on my last birthday. I took my dog to get inoculated against rabies and someone had brought an abandoned dog into the vet's to try and help it. Long story short, I ended up adopting another dog!

Nursing home (Care home) = a place where the elderly live when they are not able to look after themselves due to their age or due to an illness.

For example: There has been a lot of controversy surrounding the level of care in some nursing homes.

Topic 3. Social & Leisure

Conform = to follow social rules.

For example: I really admire my father because he refuses to conform to what society dictates. When people told him that he should go to university and study law, he refused. Instead, he started his own business when he had no money and he made it successful through hard work and effort.

Cooperate = when people work well together

For example: It's important to cooperate with your class mates because it makes projects easier and it helps you learn faster, as you can learn from each other.

Mindset (frame of mind) = the way you think. Your mental attitude at a particular point in your life or in a particular situation.

For example: When you train for an important football match, it's important to keep a positive mindset and constantly try to make small improvements. It's important to view your mistakes as lessons rather than failures.

Minority = a small percentage of a group or population.

For example: There is a minority of people who agree with this political party's policies, but the majority of the population are against them.

Shun = to reject

For example: We can't shun our responsibility as citizens. We have to be sensible and responsible to prevent dangerous situations like this from happening again.

Conventional = the usual, normal or traditional way of doing something or thinking. 'Conventional wisdom' is an expression, meaning: what most people believe to be true, or what most experts accept as the truth.

For example: I live quite a conventional life during the week. I live in a small apartment in the city centre and I work and study most days. However, at the weekends, I work as a magician at private events around the country! I love it because...........

For example: According to conventional wisdom in Hollywood, films can't make a profit unless they have big name actors and actresses and large budgets. I really like films that defy those odds, such as ...

*Note: 'defy the odds' means to succeed despite what people believe or despite low probability of success.

Interaction = communication between people (written, spoken or through sign language for example).

For example: Social media and the internet in general have changed our interactions (the way we interact).

Pressure = stress or expectations.

For example: There is too much pressure on young people today. People expect us to have everything figured out by the time we're 18, but that doesn't usually happen. I know people who are in the 40s and are still figuring their life out and deciding what they want to do!

Conduct = This can be used as verb and as a noun meaning behaviour-behave

For example: People judge you based on how you conduct yourself more than on how you dress, even though the way you dress is also a big factor.

Mainstream = common likes or ideas.

For example: My favourite band, the Snake Patrol, were not very well known when they started, but then they released that song 'Slither in the Wind' and they became mainstream. Everyone was listening to them.

Appropriate = acceptable or suitable for a particular situation.

For example: Turning up to a formal office job interview in shorts is not appropriate obviously, so they rejected him. This made him re-examine his life.

Foster = to protect something and encourage it to grow (an idea, an attitude, a feeling, an action or a result).

For example: The government has introduced policies that foster fair competition among companies.

Multicultural = something that has several different cultures. It can be a team, a department, a city, a country etc..

For example: I really want to study and work in London, because it's such a multicultural place. I love walking down the street and seeing all the different people from all over the world, or going to the markets and chatting to the locals.

Absorbing = something that entertains you so much, that you forget about everything else.

For example: The film was absorbing, I couldn't take my eyes off the screen (it had us glued to the screen). From the plot, to the characters and setting, I thought it was all incredible.

Exhilarating = something that makes you feel full of energy and excitement. Thrilling.

For example: I found paragliding exhilarating. I was hooked from the first time I tried it.

Indulge = to do something that you like (like a reward).

For example: I decided to indulge myself and had a weekend in New York.

Pursue = to follow an activity in order to reach a goal. Think of chasing your dreams.

For example: I want to pursue a career in engineering.

Tedious = not exciting. Focusing on highly specific but boring things (in the speaker's opinion).

For example: I find numbers and Maths quite tedious, I'm much more interested in biology.

Trivial = unimportant

For example: Lots of decisions that we think are really important when we're younger seem trivial when we get older.

Unwind = to begin the process of relaxation after stress or hard work

For example: I usually like to unwind by doing some exercise and meeting up with some friends at the weekend. We have a few drinks and go out for dinner or we watch a film. I also like to unwind at the end of the day by reading and listening to some music. It really helps to clear my mind.

Topic 4. Education

Theoretical = coming from theories, not practice. It's another way of saying that something has not been proven in the real world. Theoretical is also used as an adjective to describe something that focuses on abstract concepts rather than practicing a skill.

For example: The idea that time-travel is possible is purely theoretical. We don't actually know because it is currently impossible to test the theory.

For example: I think it's important to have a theoretical component in a Business course so you can understand certain concepts, but you also need a practical component so you can learn how to implement those concepts in the real world.

Acquire = to buy with money, get by chance or gain through effort.

For example: I recently acquired a new watch, which I have completely fallen in love with!

Please *Note: It's quite a formal verb, so it is often used in every day conversation with a little bit of irony. It's used as a colourful alternative to 'buy', 'get', or 'gain' in informal conversations.

In formal conversations, it's often used in interviews or speaking exams such as the IELTS test.

For example: Talk about something you've acquired recently.

You should mention:

What It is
When you acquired it.
How you acquired it
Why it's important to you.

Compulsory = obligatory, something you HAVE to do

For example: I believe that it should be compulsory to have some sort of practical training as part of your degree. I think that getting industry experience is vital in today's job market.

*Note: 'Industry experience' is a term which literally means experience of working in the sector where you want to be employed. (It can be work experience placements or full-time jobs you've had in the past)

Valid = acceptable or reasonable

For example: You make a valid point. (This means: 'What you're saying is fair').

Determine = find out or discover

For example: First, I have to determine whether I should study a Master's degree or whether I should try to gain more industry experience.

Establish = prove or consolidate

For example: They should establish where the virus came from first, and then establish ways to prevent this from happening again in the future.

Significant = meaningful or important

For example:

Talk about a significant day in your life.

You should say:

When it was.
What happened.
Why it was significant and how it made you feel.

Answer: Ok, the most meaningful/important day I can remember is ....

Miscalculation = a mistake, using bad judgment or making an error in a calculation.

For example: I think that choosing this venue for the event was a miscalculation on my part, as they were completely unprepared and didn-t offer any of the services they advertised. I really should have checked their reviews first.

Methodical = being organised or careful and patient when you do something.

For example: I think that in order to be as successful as possible at university, you need to be methodical by always keeping an organised *Notebook and by always categorising your *Notes into sections.

Cram = to overload the brain by trying to learn a lot in a short period of time.

For example: I always say that I'm going to be really organised for my tests, but I always end up cramming it all in at the last minute!

TOPIC 5: ADVERTISING

Persuade = convince someone of something For example: The role of advertising is to persuade customers to buy products they don't necessarily need.
Unavoidable = certain For example: If you allow advertisers to promote gambling, people will gamble more. It's unavoidable.
Effective = when something achieves its purpose For example: effective advertising sells products and creates brand awareness.
Ploy = trick For example: Shops use special discounts as a marketing ploy to encourage people to go into their shops and buy other products. People go into the shop for the discount and end up buying products that are not on discount.
Intrusive = invasive For example: I find intrusive advertising like internet popups and cookies really annoying.
Hype-up = exaggerate for a commercial or public relations interest

*Note: we also use 'hype' as a noun meaning exaggeration (usually for commercial reasons)

For example: It's important to ignore the hype when you're trying to choose a good restaurant.

Endorse = officially recommend a product or a company

For example: Nike are endorsed by famous professional footballers all over the world.

Gullible = too trusting or easy to trick

For example: I think we are all quite gullible as consumers. We often believe companies just because they advertise on TV.

Prominent = noticeable or extraordinary

For example: A prominent marketing guru argues that all publicity, whether it's positive or negative, is actually good for a company.

Entice = tempt by offering something

For example: Fast food companies entice us with adverts of delicious looking food, but when you actually try it, it's often disappointing.

Bombard = continuously direct something towards someone

For example: We are constantly bombarded with adverts every day on TV, online, on the radio, in newspapers and even on the street. It seems like everywhere we look there's an advert.

Inescapable = something you can't avoid.

For example: It seems like everywhere we look there's an advert, it's inescapable.

TOPIC 6: TRAVEL & PLACES

Memorable = something special or unforgettable

For example: Traveling round America with my family was a memorable experience. We managed to visit six states in total and did an amazing road trip down Route 66.

Custom = a local tradition or habit

For example: It's a custom to eat cheese and cold-cuts in Mediterranean countries such as Spain and Italy.

Remote = isolated or far away

For example: During our trip to Thailand, we visited a remote island just off the coast of Phuket. It was spectacular.

Spectacular = stunning, amazing or very impressive

For example: When I visited Bangkok, I ate the most spectacular food and the temples were absolutely stunning.

Landscape = large natural area of land

For example: The South of Spain has some amazing landscapes. In some areas, you can go skiing in the mornings and then go to the hot beach in the afternoon. It's stunning.

Basic = simple, not complicated or luxurious. (Often used to describe accommodation)

For example: Our hotel was really basic, but we only used it as a place to sleep. We spent most of our time outside, exploring the city and going on guided tours. It was an amazing experience.

Barren = without vegetation

For example: The landscape is quite barren, but it's stunningly beautiful. The sunsets in particular are amazing.

Wander = walk without a specific destination

For example: On our first day in Berlin, we wandered round the city and explored different markets and bars around the centre.

TOPIC 7: ANIMALS

Endangered = a species of animal or plant that's dying. For example: The Mountain Gorilla is one of the most critically endangered animals on the planet.
Venomous = poisonous For example: Many people assume that most snakes are poisonous, but of the 3,500 snake species around the world, only 600 are actually venomous.
Domesticated = trained to live with humans in houses instead of in the wild. For example: I think it's important to remember that not all animals can be or should be domesticated. I honestly believe that people should not be allowed to have pets like snakes, birds or monkeys. It's cruel and potentially dangerous in my opinion.
Thrive = grow strong For example: While many animals are already facing and will continue to face serious problems due to global warming, some species will actually thrive on a warming planet.
Vulnerable = something that can be hurt or that is in danger. For example: Scientists recently created the largest botanical dataset ever, and discovered that almost 40% of plant species that live on land are potentially vulnerable to

global warming. If we don't make radical changes now, we risk losing these species in the next few years. This will be carry disastrous consequences for human beings.

Dwindle = shrink in numbers, become fewer or weaker

For example: Higher penalties could stop smugglers, protect public health and help preserve dwindling species such as tigers.

Habitat = Natural environment of an animal or plant species.

For example: The large human presence in the area has had an negative effect on fish habitats.

Survival = continuing to exist

For example: We must put stricter systems in place in order to ensure the survival of species such as chimpanzees, mountain gorillas and orangutans.

Co-exist = live in the same time or place
For example: Humans can co-exist with plants and other animals, we just need to see it as a major priority. I strongly believe that in ten or twenty-years-time it will be too late to reverse the effects of global warming. We must act now; our survival depends on it.

TOPIC 8: TECHNOLOGY AND COMPUTERS

Virtual = in a computer or simulation, not in the real world

For example: I know it's a bit of a cliché, but I still believe that virtual reality is the future of entertainment.

Digital = computerised rather than physical. Often used to refer to information and information products.

For example: Sales of digital books, or e-books, have been rising steadily for years now.

Embrace = happily accept

For example: However, not everyone has embraced this new era of reading on your phone or on other electronic devices. Many people still prefer to read books the traditional way.

Addictive = when something makes people want more and more

For example: I think that as a society, we're not paying enough attention to the fact that technology is very addictive. While it can be extremely beneficial, there are also many potential drawbacks.

*Note: 'drawbacks' is like saying 'disadvantages'

Security (Secure) = Safety (Safe)

For example: Data security is a massive issue at the moment, and rightfully so. Companies hold a lot of information about us, and it would be dangerous in the wrong hands.

*Note: 'and rightfully so', is an informal expression we use at the end of sentences to state that what we've just mentioned is justified.

Examples could be: Smoking has been banned in public spaces, and rightfully so!

When they didn't send her the product she'd paid for, she demanded her money back, and rightfully so!

Cutting-edge = the newest or most advanced technology, design or method.

For example: My favourite possession is my new phone. I bought it last week. This particular model contains a cutting-edge processor which makes it 50% faster than the previous model from the same brand. I also love the design, as it's sleek and robust at the same time.

*Note: 'Sleek' means smooth or stylish, while 'robust' means strong and durable. In the example you could have also talked about its 'cutting-edge design' instead of its processor.

Cyberbullying = attacking other people online

For example: Cyberbullying is a huge issue nowadays, because victims cannot escape the bullying.

Technological = relate to technology

For example: The technological era has brought many benefits to our lives. In my opinion, it has massively improved human interaction by providing us with more options to connect with people from all over the planet and to keep in touch with family and friends when we're far away.

It has allowed us to communicate during times of crisis and it allows us to work together for common goals. None of this was possible (would have been possible) thirty years ago.

Dated = not relevant or true anymore because things have changed

For example: It would be an absolute game-changer if the government could introduce a policy of upgrading dated technology with cutting-edge energy efficient models, improving performance and energy consumption.

*Note: a 'game-changer' or 'game-changing', means a radical change (usually positive). Something that would change everything if it was applied.

Domestic appliances = machines we use in our homes

Domestic appliances are a multi-billion-dollar industry. Although many of them are extremely handy, we often end up buying devices we don't need and that don't even make our lives any easier.

*Notes: 'Handy' means convenient.
'White goods', means domestic appliances like washing machines and dishwashers, but doesn't usually include devices like blenders or air fryers for example.

Surpass = Be or do more than. Do something better than or be better than. Be bigger than, higher than, faster than etc.

For example: As humans, we continually strive to surpass what we can do and what we think is possible. I think it's mind-boggling to think about the technology we might have in 1-200 years, and the things that will be possible in 500 years. It just blows my mind!

*Note: 'mind-boggling' means 'amazing' or 'incredible'.
'It blows my mind' or it's 'mind blowing' means the same. It's something so amazing or interesting, that it excites you and makes you feel a sense of wonder.

Upgrade = get a better-quality version of something

For example: We decided to upgrade our kitchen, replacing all of our outdated appliances with new cutting-edge ones.

Innovative = creative and new

For example: I believe that some of the most innovative inventions in human history have been born out of pure necessity. It's a total cliché, but necessity really is the mother of invention.

*Note: 'Necessity is the mother of invention' is a cliché expression in English and in several other languages. It means that humans invent things they need. In times of extreme need we think of our most creative ideas in order to survive.

TOPIC 9: FASHION

Shoppers = people who buy from retail stores.

For example: Why do some people enjoy clothes shopping?

Good question! I think some shoppers enjoy the experience of walking around the different shops trying things on. Many people also go with friends or family and make it into a social outing. They go for lunch, or for coffee, or they go to the cinema after shopping.

Passing = short. Something that will disappear quickly

For example: I really hope responsible fashion isn't a passing trend. I hope that the top brands in the industry will take a more active role in the near-future, as more people recognise the importance of being environmentally-conscious.

Trendy = fashionable

For example: I believe that some people choose clothes only because they are trendy, but I don't think most people do that. I think most people choose the clothes they like within the current trends.

Impulsive = an action carried out without thinking. Or a person who doesn't think before acting.

For example: Impulsive buying is a habit that I would like to stop! Whenever I go to a shopping centre I always end up buying something. I find it really hard to resist!

Consumerism = the behaviour or culture of buying things we don't necessarily need.

For example: I think consumerism is mostly negative, because it makes us focus on things that aren't important. Many people put more time and effort into obtaining material possessions than they do into improving themselves as human beings.

Purchase = in the noun form, this means something that has been bought. In the verb form, it means 'buy'.

For example: The most memorable thing I've ever purchased is my car. It gives me independence and freedom so I can go wherever I want. It allows me to study and work and it allows me to visit my friends and family. Having it has completely changed my life for the better.

For example (verb): I had to borrow money to purchase my first car.

Topic 10: City Life

Inadequate = not good enough

For example: Half of the city's population live in inadequate housing. The conditions are quite bad for these people, as most of them don't have running water.

Transportation (transport) = the type of vehicle you use to travel

For example: Public transport in my home town is great. There are buses every fifteen minutes and train lines every twenty minutes. You can be anywhere in town within twenty minutes.

Pedestrian = person walking on the street

For example: I found Amsterdam to be very pedestrian-friendly, as there are very few cars, and the bikes there are quite respectful of the people walking around.

Commute = In the noun form, this means your journey to school or work. In the verb for, it means to travel to work or school.

For example: I have to commute for one hour every day to get to class!

Pavement = the place where pedestrians should walk on the street (not the road).

For example: The pavements are quite run-down in my neighbourhood, but the council don't have enough money to fix them.

Slums = very poor-quality housing, often without running water or electricity.

For example: One third of the people in the city live in slums. They don't have electricity or running water.

Infrastructure = services and basic structures in an area. Infra- means 'below;' so the infrastructure is the 'basic structure below' a country, an economy, a business or an organisation.

For example: More funding is required to boost the crumbling infrastructure of the country's production plants.

*Notes:
Funding = Money
Required = Needed
Boost = Improve or revitalise
Crumbling = decaying or run-down

Overpopulated (overpopulation)= when there are too many people in an area.

For example: The overpopulation in urban areas has led to an increase in pollution and inadequate housing among other issues. This is something that needs to be addressed sooner rather than later.

*Note: 'sooner rather than later' is an expression to emphasise that something needs to be done now not in the future.

Outskirts = the edge of a city, town or village.

For example: I grew up on the outskirts of the city, but I moved closer to the centre when I started working. The commute was just too long to do every day!

Isolated = separated from others

For example: When I travelled round Mexico, I visited an isolated community in the middle of the desert. It was really interesting. Most of the people there had never seen a foreigner before, so they were really curious. They were so welcoming and kind that I actually felt a bit sad when I had to leave.

Inequality = The opposite of equality. Disparity or imbalance in something. Often used to talk about people's rights or living standards.

For example: John Milton proposed a new system designed to remove inequalities in health care but it was rejected by his own political party.

Overwhelmed = unable to deal with a situation

For example: The healthcare system was initially overwhelmed by the sheer number of infections.

*Note: the word 'sheer' is used to express that the only thing that affected the situation was the thing you're talking about. In the example, 'the number of infections', the number of infections was the only or main cause of the problem.

Shortage = a lack of something

For example: Water shortages cause major problems in some areas of the country.

Affluent = rich / wealthy / prosperous

For example: I really admire my uncle Bob, because he grew up in a very deprived area, but he managed to set up several businesses and he now lives in one of the most affluent areas in town. I admire his drive and ambition, as well as his creativity.

*Notes:
Deprived= poor
Grow up= when you're raised in a certain place
Set up = start businesses or projects
Drive= Determination (refusing to be defeated)

Run-down = when talking about things it means old and neglected.

For example: Some parts of my city are quite run-down, but the centre is very nice to walk around and has........

*Note: When talking about humans, 'run-down' means tired-looking or looking slightly ill.

TOPIC 11: ENVIRONMENT

Agricultural= connected to raising animals for food and growing fruits and vegetables by cultivating the soil and producing crops.

For example: I grew up in an agricultural community so farming was still in my blood.

Renewable = something that can be produced again and again

For example: Trees are renewable natural resources, but they should be treated with extreme care.

Logging = cutting down trees

For example: Logging is a major issue in many forests and jungles all over the world. As more trees are chopped down, these natural areas are shrinking more and more.

Vital = essential for the existence of something

For example: Trees are vital for the environment.

Irrigation = systems to supply areas with water.

For example: Lack of investment in new methods may result in deterioration of the irrigation system in the area and a subsequent decline of the local economy.

*Notes:

Deterioration= decay. When something breaks down and dissolves

Subsequent= eventual. When something happens as a result of something else.

Pressing = urgent

For example: There is a pressing need for housing in the area.

Pollutant = a substance that contaminates

For example: The most dangerous gaseous air pollutants released into the air in urban areas are Sulphur dioxide, nitrogen dioxide, and carbon monoxide;

Ecosystem = the environment in an area and all the biological life in it

For example: Half of these trees could be gone within five years, threatening jobs and ecosystems.

Unprecedented = something that has never happened before

For example: Governments were not sure how to deal with the situation because it was unprecedented in 21st-century life.

Safeguard = protect against something

For example: We must safeguard the environment against the destruction of habitats and the over-exploitation of natural resources such as fresh water and fisheries among other issues.

Topic 12: Media

Tabloid = newspapers that are not as serious and impartial

For example: The President's blunders gave the tabloid press great satisfaction.

Impartial = neutral

For example: A judge has to be fair and impartial, or the law loses all meaning.

*Note: when something 'loses all meaning', we mean that it loses its purpose or value in some way.

Biased = not neutral or impartial

For example: The tabloid press gave a very biased account of the situation.

*Note: the word 'account' means 'report' in this context.

Escapism = a noun to describe when you use something to forget about normal life and escape your problems.

For example: For many people watching fantasy series and films on Netflix or on TV is a form of escapism.

Medium = singular noun for media. Media is plural (most people don't realise).

For example: Interactive series and films open up the medium of video platforms to the participation of viewers.

Well informed = having enough high-quality information to understand and make good decisions

For example: Consumers need to be well informed about the side effects of so-called natural remedies.

*Note: 'So-called' is used to communicate to the listener that you believe a word that is used to describe someone or something is wrong in some way.

Scrutinise = examine or analyse carefully

For example: It's important to scrutinise politicians to ensure that they are honest and trustworthy.

Censor = to remove parts of what is said or published in the media or in any form of communication because you don't want someone to see, read or hear that information.

For example: I completely disagree with any initiatives which aim to censor the Internet in any way, shape or form.

*Note: 'in any way, shape or form' means 'in any way', but adds extra emphasis.

Manipulate = to control someone or something indirectly (has a negative connotation)

For example: I think the government and the media manipulate us in many ways. They report the news the way they want us to see it.

Spotlight = public attention / publicity / limelight / being in the public eye

For example: I think many celebrities struggle with livn. their lives in the spotlight. It must be very hard to have every part of your life scrutinised by strangers.

Imply = to suggest something without saying it directly

For example: The media implied that there had been a cover-up. They never said it directly, but it was the logical conclusion from the way they reported the whole story.

*Note: a 'cover-up' is when governments or businesses try to stop the public from finding out about something serious.

IELTS LISTENING & READING VOCABULARY DICTIONARY

-A-

Abate: MEANING: Reduce, diminish

SENTENCE: Her stress over spending so much money on her house abated when the real estate broker told her about the property's current market value.

Aberrant: MEANING: Abnormal, deviant

SENTENCE: Running naked down the street might be considered aberrant behaviour.

Abeyance: MEANING: Temporary cessation or suspension

not happening

SENTENCE: Her thoughts of her lover were in abeyance while she studied for her exam.

Abridge: MEANING: Condense or shorten   *Abkürzung*

SENTENCE: Audio books are almost always abridged, since few people want to listen to a 200-hour story.

Abscond: MEANING: Leave secretly and hurriedly, often to escape or avoid arrest   *flüchten*

SENTENCE: The tenants absconded owing six months' rent.

Abstemious: MEANING: Consuming moderately in something, especially food and drink

SENTENCE: 'We only had one course at dinner.' 'Very abstemious of you.'

Abstruse: MEANING: Difficult to understand

SENTENCE: The doctor's handwriting was so abstruse that the patient had to ask him to print the letter.

Admonish: MEANING: Reprimand, warn

SENTENCE: She admonished him for pouring a third glass of wine.

Adulterate: MEANING: Debase a substance by adding another substance

SENTENCE: Cocaine is adulterated and dangerous.

Aesthetic: MEANING: Concerned with beauty

SENTENCE: There are practical as well as aesthetic reasons for planting trees; not only do trees give oxygen needed for human and animal life, but they also add beauty.

Affability: MEANING: A tendency to be friendly and approachable

SENTENCE: John's affability helped him in his interview with the Fulbright Scholarship decision panel; they selected him for the scholarship.

Affluent: MEANING: Wealthy, well off

SENTENCE: Judging by the size of the houses and the abundance of trees, this was an affluent suburb.

Aggrandize: MEANING: Increase in power, wealth, rank; or enlarge, e.g. aggrandize an estate.

SENTENCE: Some political leaders may aim to aggrandize their power without considering the wishes of their own political party.

Aggregate: MEANING: Gather into a mass or whole; accumulation of a whole

SENTENCE: The aggregate wealth of this country is staggering to the imagination.

Alacrity: MEANING: Speedy willingness

SENTENCE: He demonstrated his eagerness to cooperate by answering the email with alacrity.

Alleviate: MEANING: Lessen a problem or suffering

SENTENCE: The stimulus package has alleviated the problems of the Great Recession, but times are still tough.

Alluring: MEANING: Highly attractive, fascinating

SENTENCE: The music coming from the darkened bar was very alluring to the travellers.

Amalgam: MEANING: A mixture of multiple things

SENTENCE: The music played by the band was an amalgam of hip-hop, flamenco and jazz, blending the three styles with surprising results.

Ambiguous: MEANING: not clear or decided

SENTENCE: The election result was ambiguous.

Ambivalent: MEANING: having mixed emotions about something

SENTENCE: Sam was ambivalent about studying for the exam because doing so was time-consuming, yet he was able to improve his analytical skills.

Ameliorate: MEANING: To make better   a bad , unpleasant
                                              situation better

SENTENCE: Isabel's pain of scoring less in the exam than Kate was ameliorated when she discovered she still qualified for the Fulbright Scholarship.

Anachronism: MEANING: An error in chronology; something out of date or old-fashioned

SENTENCE: it is an anachronism to see a horse and cart on the freeway.

Analogous: MEANING: Comparable, similar

SENTENCE: Living with a pet is analogous to having a young child; you have to watch what they put into their mouth.

Anarchy: MEANING: Absence of law or government

SENTENCE: Once the dictator was assassinated, the country fell into total anarchy, as none of the opposition groups were strong enough to seize power.

Anomaly: MEANING: Deviation from what is common; something which is unusual

SENTENCE: While the cosmetics division of the company has many female executives, it's an anomaly – in the rest of the company, sadly, only 4% of management positions are filled by women.

Antipathy: MEANING: A feeling of dislike or aversion

SENTENCE: There was widespread public antipathy towards inserting an identifying chip into the vaccine.

Antiquity: MEANING: Ancient times

SENTENCE: Gold antiquities were discovered in Pakistan; these belonged to some thousand years ago.

Apathy: MEANING: Lack of concern, motivation or interest in important matters

SENTENCE: As a firm believer in democratic government, she could not understand the apathy of people who never bothered to vote.

Appease: MEANING: Satisfy and relieve

SENTENCE: My mother is so angry she wasn't the first person we called when the baby was born – I'm hoping to appease her by bringing the baby to see her today!

Apprise: MEANING: Inform or tell (someone)

SENTENCE: I thought it was the right thing to apprise Chris of what had happened in his office while he was away.

Approbation: MEANING: approval or praise

SENTENCE: He wrote many approbations to works of Hebrew literature.

Appropriate: MEANING: suitable or proper in the circumstances

SENTENCE: It was entirely appropriate that she brought her boyfriend to the family Christmas party.

Arcane: MEANING: Secret, mysterious, known only to the initiated

SENTENCE: Cursive writing is becoming arcane in our world of word processing.

Arduous: MEANING: Requiring lots of hard work, very difficult

SENTENCE: Without a proper teacher, the exam is far too arduous to study for by yourself.

Articulate: MEANING: Using language in a clear, fluent way

SENTENCE: Her articulate presentation of the advertising campaign impressed her employers.

Artless: MEANING: Natural, without pretence or deception

SENTENCE: Many people believe that Imran Khan seems to be an artless politician who can eliminate corruption from Pakistan.

Ascetic: MEANING: Practising pronounced self-discipline from all forms of indulgence

SENTENCE: Religious people can live frugal and ascetic lives.

Assiduous: MEANING: Showing great care and perseverance

SENTENCE: She was assiduous in pointing out every feature of the home to the prospective buyers.

Assuage: MEANING: Provide relief from an unpleasant feeling

SENTENCE: The electricity supply finally resumed, and it assuaged the angry people; because after a few minutes they forgot their inconvenience.

Attenuate: MEANING: Reduce the force, effect, or value of

SENTENCE: Many people claim that the flu vaccine attenuates their illness.

Audacious: MEANING: Daring, bold; taking risks

SENTENCE: She made an audacious decision to quit her job.

Auspicious: MEANING: Favourable, positive

SENTENCE: The opening night of the musical received an auspicious review from the theatre critic.

Austere: MEANING: Severely simple, plain

SENTENCE: The graduation speaker Delivered an austere message: the economy Is bad, and academic success alone isn't enough to succeed in the job market.

Austerity: MEANING: Sternness, severity; reduced public spending

During the recession, the government introduced austerity measures, and many public servants were retrenched.

Autonomous: MEANING: Independent

SENTENCE: The country was comprised of a number of autonomous provinces.

Avarice: MEANING: Greed for wealth

SENTENCE: Early gold-diggers were inspired by avarice.

Avid: MEANING: Passionate or enthusiastic

SENTENCE: Hamid Is an avid reader of novels, articles and editorials; this helped his comprehension immensely.

-B -

Banal: MEANING: Lacking originality

SENTENCE: Frequent use of ordinary and uninteresting words makes an essay seem banal; this generates a low score in essays.

Belie: MEANING: Give a false impression

SENTENCE: The corrupt actions of some officials belie their claim to be representative of sound authority.

Beneficent: MEANING: (of a person) generous or doing good

SENTENCE: Clarissa found a beneficent mentor in her manager at work.

Benign: MEANING: Harmless

The doctor told Stephen that the lump on his arm was benign and could be removed easily.

Bracing: MEANING: Fresh, invigorating; giving strength

SENTENCE: Heather took her dog for a bracing walk by the ocean at 6am that day.

Burgeon: MEANING: Grow rapidly, flourish

SENTENCE: In the spring, the plants that burgeon are a promise of the beauty that is to come.

Burnish: MEANING: enhance or improve

SENTENCE: The politician took advantage of any opportunity to burnish his image.

Bolster: MEANING: Support or strengthen

SENTENCE: The fall in interest rates is starting to bolster investor confidence.

Bombastic: MEANING: Pompous, showy

SENTENCE: The speech made by the new headmaster was a little bombastic.

Boorish: MEANING: rough and bad-mannered; coarse.

SENTENCE: Even though the pirate captain was brutal and boorish with his men, he was always courteous to the female captives.

Buttress: MEANING: Support, reinforce

SENTENCE: In the debating club, the students learnt how to buttress their argument with relevant facts.

- C -

Cacophony: MEANING: A harsh, discordant, or meaningless mixture of sounds.

SENTENCE: The noise of barking dogs and sirens added to the cacophony at midnight; I didn't sleep.

Candid: MEANING: Sincere or honest

SENTENCE: The candid attitude of the prime minister inspired many young individuals to see him as a role model.

Capricious: MEANING: Unpredictable

SENTENCE: Share market behaviour was capricious during the COVID-19 pandemic.

Castigate: MEANING: Criticize harshly

SENTENCE: Drill sergeants are known to castigate new recruits so mercilessly that the latter often break down.

Chicanery: MEANING: The use of deception or subterfuge

SENTENCE: There is plenty of chicanery in the world of international espionage.

Catalyst: MEANING: Something that causes change

SENTENCE: The student's ideas were the catalyst for the teacher's different approach to teaching.

Caustic: MEANING: Intended to hurt, bitterly sarcastic

SENTENCE: The divorcing couple spoke to each other with caustic remarks.

Circumscribe: MEANING: Limit or restrict

SENTENCE: Unreliable access to funds circumscribed the investor's activities.

Coagulate: MEANING: (of a fluid) change to a solid or semi-solid state

SENTENCE: Blood had coagulated around the edges of the wound.

Chauvinism: MEANING: Excessive support for one's own cause, group or sex

SENTENCE: Male chauvinists do not believe women are their equal.

Coda: MEANING: A concluding event, section or remark

SENTENCE: A prayer was the coda to the priest's session that Sunday.

Cogent: MEANING: Convincing, logical

SENTENCE: The defence presented cogent arguments to the jury; their verdict: not guilty.

Commensurate: MEANING: Equal in extent, proportional

SENTENCE: Her salary was commensurate with her experience and qualifications.

Compendium: MEANING: a collection or set of similar items.

SENTENCE: The book she borrowed was a compendium of maps and stories of the country she planned to visit.

Complaisant: MEANING: Willing to please others

SENTENCE: Flight attendants are usually very complaisant with passengers.

Condone: MEANING: Accept or overlook behaviour that is considered wrong or offensive

SENTENCE: The school did not condone smoking in the playground.

Confound: MEANING: Cause confusion with surprise; mix up

SENTENCE: The twins would deliberately confound their teachers by swapping seats in the classroom.

Connoisseur: MEANING: Expert of art; or simply, expert

SENTENCE: Miguel managed a vineyard and was something of a wine connoisseur.

Compliant: MEANING: Submissive, willing to obey someone else

SENTENCE: He was compliant when the police asked him to step out of the car.

Contentious: MEANING: Likely to cause controversy

SENTENCE: The filmmaker produced a very contentious documentary on the state of the global environment.

Conciliatory: MEANING: Soothing and satisfying

SENTENCE: She was still angry despite his conciliatory words to her after their argument.

Contrite: MEANING: Feeling or expressing remorse

SENTENCE: The teacher found a very contrite student when he visited the detention room.

Concomitant: MEANING: Accompanying, associated

SENTENCE: The joys of motherhood had concomitant anxieties.

Conundrum: MEANING: A difficult problem; puzzle

SENTENCE: The study of physics involved many conundrums.

Converge: MEANING: Tending to come together from different directions

SENTENCE: The crowd converged on the holy relic.

Convoluted: MEANING: Twisted, very complicated

SENTENCE: Your argument is so convoluted that I'm not able to understand it enough to start critiquing it.

Courteous: MEANING: Polite and respectful in manner

SENTENCE: The lawyer sent me a very courteous letter.

Craven: MEANING: Very cowardly

SENTENCE: When he saw the enemy troops advancing, he had a craven impulse to run for his life.

Crestfallen: MEANING: Dejected, sad and disappointed

SENTENCE: Half the crowd in the stadium were crestfallen after their team lost the grand final.

Culpability: MEANING: Deserving blame

SENTENCE: The extent of the culpability of each nation in its handling of the crisis became clearer over time.

Cursory: MEANING: Brief, hasty

SENTENCE: He gave the report a cursory glance before handing it to his secretary.

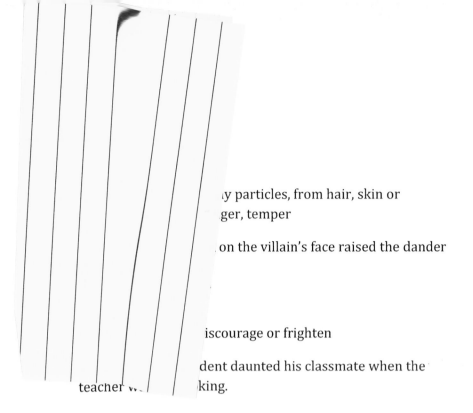

y particles, from hair, skin or

ger, temper

on the villain's face raised the dander

iscourage or frighten

dent daunted his classmate when the

teacher w̲   king.

Credulous: MEANING: Trusting too easily or without enough evidence.

SENTENCE: Few people are credulous enough to believe that the United Nations has global authority.

Debunk: MEANING: Show something to be false

SENTENCE: Investigative journalists have debunked various political myths.

Decorum: MEANING: Proper In manners and conduct

SENTENCE: Discipline requires the decorum of one's behaviour and attitude towards rules and regulations.

Default: MEANING: Failure to fulfil an obligation, especially a financial one

SENTENCE: The company will have to restructure its debts to avoid default.

Deference: MEANING: Polite and respectful submission

SENTENCE: He responded with natural deference, giving them his full attention.

Deliberation: MEANING: Careful consideration; slow movement

SENTENCE: The jury delivered its verdict after due deliberation.

Delineate: MEANING: Describe in precise detail

SENTENCE: I do need the cash, but I'm not signing up for this psychological experiment unless you delineate what's going to happen.

Demean: MEANING: Cause a loss in dignity and respect for something or someone; do something that is beneath one's dignity

SENTENCE: She did not demean herself by calling her boyfriend after seeing him with another girl.

Denigrate: MEANING: Criticize unfairly; disparage.

SENTENCE: Don't listen to the doom and gloom merchants who denigrate their own country.

Deride: MEANING: Express contempt for; ridicule.

SENTENCE: The decision to create a shopping mall in front of the lake was derided by environmentalists

Derivative: MEANING: Not original

SENTENCE: Many modern singers' albums are mere disappointment, derivative of several hit albums from past legends.

Desiccate: MEANING: Dehydrate, remove water from

SENTENCE: Out West, it was the time of the summer sun and dust storms, when whole desiccated farms blew away.

Desultory: MEANING: Lacking a plan, purpose, or enthusiasm

SENTENCE: A few people were left at the party, dancing in a desultory fashion.

Deterrent: MEANING: something that discourages or is intended to discourage someone from doing something

SENTENCE: Cameras are a major deterrent to crime

Diatribe: MEANING: A forceful and bitter verbal attack against someone or something

SENTENCE: The speech was a diatribe against consumerism.

Dichotomy: MEANING: A contrast between two things that are opposed, or very different.

SENTENCE: There is a fixed dichotomy between science and religion.

Didacticism: MEANING: A philosophy of teaching in art and literature

SENTENCE: The didactic qualities of his poetry overshadow its literary qualities; the lesson he teaches is more memorable than the lines.

Diffidence: MEANING: Lack of self-confidence, shyness

SENTENCE: Her diffidence showed up in the classroom when she was asked to speak.

Diffuse: MEANING: Spread out over a large area; not concentrated

SENTENCE: New technologies diffuse rapidly.

Digression: MEANING: a temporary departure from the main subject in speech or writing.

SENTENCE: "Let's return to the main topic after that brief digression."

Disabuse: MEANING: Free somebody from an incorrect belief.

SENTENCE: I will attempt to disabuse you of your impression of my client's guilt; I know he is innocent.

Discerning: MEANING: Mentally quick and observant

SENTENCE: The ships in the harbour were not discernible in the fog.

Discordant: MEANING: Disagreeing or incongruous; lacking in harmony

SENTENCE: The operative principle of democracy is a balance of discordant qualities

Discountenance: MEANING: Refuse to approve of; disturb the composure of

SENTENCE: When capitalist development discountenances the people, it loses its soul. The soul of capitalist development at the national, regional and global level must be the people.

Discredit: MEANING: Injure The reputation of

SENTENCE: the campaign was highly negative in tone; each candidate tried to discredit the other.

Discrepancy: MEANING: Lack of consistency between facts

SENTENCE: There is a discrepancy between the accountant's report and the client's.

Dirge: MEANING: A mournful song, piece of music, or sound

SENTENCE: When Kim sang a dirge for her deceased father, she brought everyone to tears.

Discrete: MEANING: Individually separate

SENTENCE: Speech is produced as a continuous sound signal rather than discrete units.

Disingenuous: MEANING: Not sincere, not simple

SENTENCE: Although he was young, his remarks indicated that he was disingenuous.

Disinterested: MEANING: Unprejudiced by consideration of personal gain; uninterested.

SENTENCE: My decision to invest in your company is a disinterested one; I am acting on behalf of a client.

Disjointed: MEANING: Disconnected

SENTENCE: In politics we have seen, whenever there is a clash of interests, political parties have become disjointed.

Dismiss: MEANING: Discharge from an office or position; treat as unworthy of consideration

SENTENCE: The prime minister dismissed five members of his cabinet.

Disparage: MEANING: Belittle, regard as being of little worth

SENTENCE: The feminist group tended to disparage men.

Disparate: MEANING: Essentially different, not able to be compared.

SENTENCE: The two authors inhabit disparate worlds of thought.

Disquieting: MEANING: Disturbing, causing anxiety.

SENTENCE: Mr. Amir's lack of emotion at his wife's death was disquieting – so much so, in fact, that even his own family began to suspect he had something to do with it.

Dissemble: MEANING: Hide or disguise one's real feelings or beliefs

SENTENCE: She smiled and looked away, dissembling her true emotions.

Disseminate: MEANING: Spread widely, especially information

SENTENCE: Health authorities should foster good practice by disseminating information

Dissolution: MEANING: the action of ceasing or dismissing an assembly, partnership, or official body

SENTENCE: The dissolution of their marriage after 20 years took place in a few minutes.

Dissonance: MEANING: lack of agreement or harmony, especially in music

SENTENCE: The meeting ended in uproar and dissonance.

Distend: MEANING: Swell or cause to swell by pressure from inside

SENTENCE: The abdomen distended rapidly.

Distil: MEANING: Remove impurities from, increase the concentration of

SENTENCE: You can't drink the water from the river, but you can distil it.

Divest: MEANING: Take something away from somebody

SENTENCE: The president was divested of his power to act and could no longer govern.

Doctrinaire: MEANING: Trying to impose doctrine without taking practical considerations into account

SENTENCE: Mr. Chief Justice is such a doctrinaire person that he will never compromise on the sentences he makes for terrorists.

Document: MEANING: Support with evidence; written piece

SENTENCE: In the analytical writing assessment, if you write an essay with well-documented examples, you should get a high score.

Dogmatic: MEANING: inclined to lay down principles as undeniably true

SENTENCE: She was not tempted to be too dogmatic about what she believed.

Dogmatism: MEANING: The tendency to be right all the time, with little consideration for others

SENTENCE: Mr. Jones shows an inflexible dogmatism when it comes to answering difficult questions.

Dormant: MEANING: Temporarily inactive

SENTENCE: The disease may remain dormant and undetected until it is transmitted to other fish.

Dupe: MEANING: Trick, deceive

SENTENCE: The manager was duped into hiring a criminal.

- E -

Ebullient: MEANING: Energetic and full of cheer

SENTENCE: Fatima sounded ebullient and happy when she got very high exam score.

Eccentric: MEANING: Odd; deviating from normal, unusual

SENTENCE: Her parents were eccentric but very lovable.

Eclectic: MEANING: Selecting what seems best from various styles or ideas

SENTENCE: The government applied a set of bipartisan and eclectic policies.

Efficacy: MEANING: The quality of being able to produce the intended effect

SENTENCE: The efficacy of your preparation of the exam depends on your devotion and hard work.

Effrontery: MEANING: Rude or impertinent behaviour

SENTENCE: The teacher condones no effrontery in her classroom.

Egregious: MEANING: Extremely bad to such an extent that it becomes shocking

SENTENCE: The prime minister's abuse of power was so egregious that even his own family deserted him and asked the international courts to take action against him.

Elegy: MEANING: a mournful poem; a lament for the dead

SENTENCE: An example of an elegy is a poem written to honour a deceased man

Elicit: MEANING: Draw out a reaction, answer, or fact

SENTENCE: I tried to elicit a smile from Joanna.

Eloquence: MEANING: Persuasive speech or writing

SENTENCE: She spoke with such eloquence at the meeting.

Embellish: MEANING: Decorate and adorn; add details to a story that may not be accurate

SENTENCE: My mother-in-law's stories about her journey from Russia made us laugh because she embellished the bare facts of her travels with humorous anecdotes.

Empirical: MEANING: Based on experience or experimentation

SENTENCE: He distrusted hunches and intuitive flashes; he placed his reliance entirely on empirical data.

Emulate: MEANING: Imitate; match or surpass by imitation

SENTENCE: Many singers wished to emulate Elvis Presley.

Endemic: MEANING:) Regularly found among particular people or in a certain area (of a disease or condition)

SENTENCE: Is surging inequality endemic to capitalism?

Enervate: MEANING: To weaken physically, mentally or morally

SENTENCE: The long suffering from paralysis has enervated him.

Engender: MEANING: Give rise to, cause (a feeling, situation, or condition)

SENTENCE: The issue of race raised by the politician has engendered continuing controversy.

Enhance: MEANING: Further improve the quality, value, or extent of; intensify, increase

SENTENCE: His refusal does nothing to enhance his reputation.

Ephemeral: MEANING: Lasting only a short time

SENTENCE: The mayfly is an ephemeral creature; it only lives for a couple of hours.

Equanimity: MEANING: Calmness and composure, especially in difficult situations

SENTENCE: She accepted both the good and the bad with equanimity.

Equitable: MEANING: Impartial or fair

SENTENCE: The mediator suggested an equitable solution for both parties.

Equivocate: MEANING: To speak vaguely so as to conceal the truth

SENTENCE: After Sharon brought the car home an hour after her curfew, she equivocated when her parents pointedly asked her where she had been.

Erroneous: MEANING: Wrong, incorrect

SENTENCE: I thought my answer was correct, but it was erroneous; it's usually the case for tricky questions.

Erudite: MEANING: Well-educated, having or showing great knowledge or learning

SENTENCE: Steve turned any conversation into an erudite discussion.

Esoteric: MEANING: Understood by only a few people with specialized knowledge or interests; obscure

SENTENCE: She read a compilation of esoteric philosophical theories.

Eulogy: MEANING: Expression of praise, often on the occasion of someone's death.

SENTENCE: All the eulogies of his friends were read in church and the funeral was attended by many.

Euphemism: MEANING: an expression substituted for one considered to be too blunt when referring to something unpleasant or embarrassing

SENTENCE: The phrase 'passed away' is a euphemism for saying someone died.

Euphoria: MEANING: A feeling of extreme excitement

SENTENCE: Katie was euphoric after she got an admission at Harvard University, with full scholarship.

Exacerbate: MEANING: Make worse

SENTENCE: The cream the doctor prescribed only exacerbated the rash on Steve's foot.

Exacting: MEANING: Extremely demanding

SENTENCE: The author's requirements were exacting, the editor would need weeks to do the work.

Exculpate: MEANING: Show someone is free from blame

SENTENCE: I will present evidence of innocence and honesty in his 10 years of service for this country that will exculpate my client from such groundless charges.

Exigency: MEANING: Urgent requirement or need

SENTENCE: Political decisions are presented as a matter of exigency, as though there were no other choice.

Exonerate: MEANING: Officially absolve from blame; release from obligation or duty

SENTENCE: In order to work in the USA, one requires proof of exoneration from any criminal act.

Extraneous: MEANING: Irrelevant; of external origin

SENTENCE: We create bubbles of information, silos of opinion, and we tune out all that is extraneous or disagreeable.

Extrapolation: MEANING: The action of estimating by extension of current trends, or applying current methods

SENTENCE: I extrapolate that getting home will take 20 minutes as it took 20 minutes to get there.

- F -

Facetious: MEANING: Inappropriately funny, flippant

SENTENCE: Facetious remarks about a classmate are inappropriate at the serious moment when you got an excellent score in the exam, but your classmate got a very poor score.

Facile: MEANING: Superficial, simplistic; easily achieved

SENTENCE: His essay contained many facile generalizations.

Facilitate: MEANING: Make an action or process easier.

SENTENCE: Businesses were located in the same area to facilitate the residents' visiting and shopping.

Fallacious: MEANING: Based on unsound arguments

SENTENCE: Don't be misled by the fallacious advertisement.

Faltering: MEANING: Hesitating; losing strength or momentum

SENTENCE: The surprising decrease in the value of the euro as compared to other currencies is sign of a faltering economy.

Fastidious: MEANING: Giving very careful attention to detail

SENTENCE: The Professor is so fastidious that he hardly ever approves a student's thesis on first submission, because he is so fastidious about little points like punctuation.

Fatuous: MEANING: Silly, foolish

SENTENCE: Her comments on the film festival competition were fatuous.

Fawning: MEANING: Showing exaggerated affection or flattery; obsequious

SENTENCE: The puppy was fawning on its master.

Felicitous: MEANING: Apt, suited to the circumstances; pleasing

SENTENCE: The felicitous music made me happy.

Fervor: MEANING: Intense and earnest feeling

SENTENCE: The priest delivered his sermon with great fervor.

Flag: MEANING: Lose enthusiasm or energy

SENTENCE: When the opposing hockey team scored its third goal only minutes into the first period, the home team's spirits flagged.

Fledgling: MEANING: a person, creature or organization that is immature, inexperienced, or underdeveloped

SENTENCE: Pakistan is a country with a fledgling democracy

Flout: MEANING: Openly disregard, in terms of a rule, law, or convention

SENTENCE: They hugged each other, openly flouting the social distancing rules.

Foible: MEANING: Slight flaw or defect, especially of character

SENTENCE: Her tendency to gossip was an all-too-human foible.

Foment: MEANING: To instigate or stir up, especially discord or trouble

SENTENCE: Greenpeace fomented protests on the ocean against whaling.

Forestall: MEANING: To prevent, hinder or thwart by action in advance

SENTENCE: They will hand in their resignations to forestall a vote of no confidence.

Forlorn: MEANING: Sad And lonely

SENTENCE: After his lover left him and went with some other guy, Edward was forlorn.

Fortuitous: MEANING: Occurring by happy chance; by lucky accident

SENTENCE: There is no connection between these two events; their timing is entirely fortuitous.

Frugality: MEANING: The attitude of not spending much money

SENTENCE: Monte was no miser, but was simply frugal, wisely spending the little that he earned.

Futile: MEANING: Useless, ineffective

SENTENCE: His attempts at scaling the wall were futile, it was simply too high for him.

- G -

Gainsay: MEANING: Deny or dispute; oppose

SENTENCE: He shrugged his shoulders, unable to gainsay the argument.

Galling: MEANING: Causing irritation, exasperating

SENTENCE: Learning vocabulary lists without sentence examples Is a galling thing for most students.

Gambit: MEANING: Action aimed at producing a future advantage; a remark to open or redirect a conversation

SENTENCE: One gambit is to require photo identification. This should ensure tenants are properly managed.

Garrulous: MEANING: Talkative, wordy

SENTENCE: Many club members avoided the company of the garrulous junior executive, because his constant chatter bored them to tears.

Gauche: MEANING: Clumsy and awkward in social behaviour

SENTENCE: It Is terribly gauche to put ketchup on your steak and then talk with your mouth full as you eat it! That's the last time I ever bring you to a nice place!

Gawky: MEANING: Physically awkward

SENTENCE: As a teenager, she thought of herself as gawky and often slouched so as not to seem so much taller than her peers; of course, now that she's a supermodel, no one thinks of her as gawky at all.

Glib: MEANING: Fluent with insincerity or superficiality

SENTENCE: Politicians are usually glib and articulate speakers; this helps them in their campaign.

Gloating: MEANING: Smug or malicious satisfaction

SENTENCE: After the fight, the winner stood over his opponent and gloated.

Goad: MEANING: Prod, incite, so as to stimulate an action or reaction.

SENTENCE: He was trying to goad her into a fight.

Gouge: MEANING: To scoop out and make grooves or holes

SENTENCE: The water channel had been gouged out by the ebbing water

Grandiloquent: MEANING: Expressed in lofty language, style, or manner, especially in a way that is intended to impress.

SENTENCE: The fiesta was a grandiloquent celebration of Spanish glory.

Gregarious: MEANING: Sociable, friendly

SENTENCE: As a gregarious boy Dave ran up to every person on the playground and wanted to be their friend.

Grovelling: MEANING: Behaving in a fawning or servile manner

SENTENCE: Journalists like to describe political leaders as grovelling in their interactions with others.

Guileless: MEANING: Innocent and without deception

SENTENCE: The student gave a guileless explanation of his absence from class.

Gullible: MEANING: Easily persuaded to believe something; credulous

SENTENCE: The plan was a deliberate attempt to persuade a gullible public to spend their money.

- H -

Hackneyed: MEANING: Commonplace, not fresh or original

SENTENCE: The English teacher criticized her story because of its hackneyed and unoriginal plot.

Halcyon: MEANING: Calm; rich; happy

SENTENCE: There were halcyon days all summer.

Harangue: MEANING: A long verbal attack; pompous speech

SENTENCE: The speaker on the soapbox harangued the government.

Harrowing: MEANING: Extremely disturbing or distressing

SENTENCE: The trip in the ambulance was harrowing for them both.

Hodgepodge: MEANING: Jumble of different kinds of things

SENTENCE: The exhibition was a hodgepodge of mediocre art, bad art, and really bad art; it was disliked by many visitors.

Homogeneous: MEANING: of the same kind; alike

SENTENCE: The unemployed are not a homogenous group.

Humdrum: MEANING: Boring, monotonous, routine

SENTENCE: After five years in the same role, Sandra found the work a little humdrum.

Hyperbole: MEANING: Exaggeration

SENTENCE: Oh, come on, saying 'that movie was so bad it made me puke,' was surely hyperbole. I strongly doubt that you actually vomited!

- I -

Iconoclastic: MEANING: Defying tradition

SENTENCE: Jackson Pollack was an iconoclastic artist, totally breaking with tradition by splashing paint on a blank canvas.

Idolatry: MEANING: The worship of idols; excessive admiration

SENTENCE: We must not allow our idolatry of pop stars to make them seem more than mortal.

Ignominious: MEANING: Embarrassing, humiliating

SENTENCE: He suffered an ignominious defeat.

Immutable: MEANING: Unchanging over time, permanent

SENTENCE: Science presents us with some immutable facts, like gravity on planet Earth.

Impair: MEANING: Make worse, damage

SENTENCE: Listening to loud music without earplugs with almost certainly impair your hearing over time.

Impassive: MEANING: Not showing emotion

SENTENCE: His cold, impassive face stared at the cripple begging on the street.

Impede: MEANING: Block or obstruct progress

SENTENCE: The judge determined that the detective had not intentionally set out to impede the progress of the investigation.

Impermeable: MEANING: Not allowing fluid to pass through, waterproof

SENTENCE: The boat is made from impermeable wood.

Imperturbable: MEANING: Unshakeably calm

SENTENCE: Greg remained imperturbable during his exam, even the last moments before completion didn't panic him.

Impervious: MEANING: Not affected or influenced; resistant to water or heat

SENTENCE: The system remained impervious to all suggestions of change.

Implacable: MEANING: Hostile, unable to be appeased, relentless

SENTENCE: The barrister was implacable in his handling of the offence.

Implicit: MEANING: Not directly expressed; essentially connected with; absolute

SENTENCE: She had an implicit faith in God.

Implode: MEANING: Burst Inward

SENTENCE: There is a new technology of controlled demolition during which old buildings implode in a matter of seconds, without any damage to nearby buildings.

Inadvertently: MEANING: Accidentally, without intention

SENTENCE: Chris inadvertently dialled Sandra's number and she happily answered the call.

Incensed: MEANING: Extremely angry

SENTENCE: Mr. Smith is known for his kindness towards children; unkindness towards children by others incensed him.

Incessantly: MEANING: Continuing without stopping

SENTENCE: The batsman hit boundaries and sixes incessantly and won the game!

Inchoate: MEANING: Just begun, not fully developed; rudimentary

SENTENCE: The country was a still inchoate democracy.

Incongruity: MEANING: Mismatch; incompatibility

SENTENCE: The incongruity of his fleshy face and skinny body disturbed her.

Inconsequential: MEANING: Having little importance; illogical; haphazard

SENTENCE: Her answers were inconsequential despite the numbering on the page.

Incorporate: MEANING: Bring something into a larger whole; include

SENTENCE: The second division team incorporated third division players in the latter half of the season.

Incorrigible: MEANING: A person or behaviour that cannot be reformed or changed

SENTENCE: My friend's father is an incorrigible drinker.

Indefatigable: MEANING: Tirelessly persisting

SENTENCE: He had courage, a vivid sense of duty, an indefatigable love of work, and all the inquisitive zeal and inventive energy of a born reformer.

Indeterminate: MEANING: Vague and unclear, cannot be determined

SENTENCE: Our galaxy has an indeterminate number of stars

Indifferent: MEANING: Not caring, unconcerned; mediocre

SENTENCE: Because she felt no desire to marry, she was indifferent to the constant proposals by her lover.

Indigence: MEANING: A state of extreme poverty; destitution

SENTENCE: After the U.S. Supreme Court case, Gideon v. Wainwright in 1963, state governments were required to provide lawyers to indigent defendants.

Indolent: MEANING: Lazy, wanting to avoid effort or exertion

SENTENCE: At lunchtime the indolent kids sat around while the active kids played games.

Ineluctable: MEANING: Inescapable, unable to be avoided

SENTENCE: Two ineluctable facts of life are death and taxes.

Inert: MEANING: Not able to move; inactive

SENTENCE: The story was inert and careless, as if the author was writing half-asleep.

Inexorable: MEANING: Continuing without any possibility of being stopped

SENTENCE: Technology moves inexorably towards a digital future.

Inherent: MEANING: Existing as a permanent, essential quality

SENTENCE: New research seems to support the idea that humans have an inherent sense of fairness – even babies become upset at equal and unequal distributions of food.

Innocuous: MEANING: Harmless, inoffensive

SENTENCE: The journalist asked a couple of innocuous questions at the press conference.

Insatiable: MEANING: Unable to be satisfied, physically and spiritually

SENTENCE: She has an insatiable desire to learn the English language.

Inscrutability: MEANING: The quality of being impossible to investigate

SENTENCE: There is a certain inscrutability of the future.

Insensible: MEANING: Barely able to be perceived; incapable of sensation

SENTENCE: There was an insensible change in his temperature.

Insinuate: MEANING: Hint at something negative; become involved in a subtle way

SENTENCE: He insinuated himself into the conversation of the people at the nearby table.

Insipid: MEANING: Lacking flavour, weak or tasteless

SENTENCE: The first band to play at the concert was a little insipid.

Insularity: MEANING: The quality of being isolated or detached

SENTENCE: The 1950s were a decade of conservatism and insularity.

Intractable: MEANING: Difficult to manage or mould

SENTENCE: The kindergarten kids were intractable and the teacher grew frustrated.

Intransigence: MEANING: Unwillingness to change one' beliefs; stubbornness

SENTENCE: Despite many calls for mercy, the judge remained intransigent, citing strict legal precedence.

Inundate: MEANING: Quickly fill up, overwhelm

SENTENCE: Her inbox was inundated with emails on her birthday.

Inured: MEANING: Made tough by habitual exposure

SENTENCE: He was inured to the sound of his neighbour's dog barking.

Invective: MEANING: Insulting, abusive, or highly critical language

SENTENCE: His invective was overheard by everyone in the next office.

Involved: MEANING: Connected; highly complex

SENTENCE: She was involved in animal care through her Girl Guides membership.

Irascible: MEANING: Having or showing a tendency to be easily angered.

SENTENCE: Early in their marriage, Julie discovered her husband could be irascible.

Irresolute: MEANING: Uncertain how to act or proceed

SENTENCE: The new governor was irresolute; he needed the advice from the committee.

Itinerary: MEANING: A planned route or journey

SENTENCE: His itinerary included an official visit to Canada

- L -

Lacklustre: MEANING: Lacking energy, excitement, enthusiasm, or passion.

SENTENCE: We were disappointed by the lacklustre performance of our cricket team this weekend.

Laconic: MEANING: Saying very little

SENTENCE: While Martha always swooned over the hunky, laconic types in romantic comedies, her boyfriend was very talkative – and not very hunky.

Largesse: MEANING: Liberality in bestowing gifts; generous of spirit

SENTENCE: Her partner's largesse warmed her heart; he was generous to family, friends and neighbours.

Lassitude: MEANING: Tiredness, laziness

SENTENCE: As a couch potato I turn lassitude into an art form!

Latent: MEANING: Existing, but not yet developed or manifest; hidden or concealed.

SENTENCE: Australia has a huge reserve of latent talent.

Laud: MEANING: Praise highly

SENTENCE: In the newspaper obituary, she was lauded as a brilliant opera singer.

Lethargic: MEANING: Affected by lethargy; sluggish and apathetic

SENTENCE: Yesterday I felt lethargic and stayed at home; today I am rearing to go!

Levee: MEANING: An embankment built to prevent the overflow of a river

SENTENCE: They had their picnic on the levee next to the river.

Levity: MEANING: Lacking seriousness

SENTENCE: Stop giggling and wriggling around in the pew; such levity is improper in church.

Log: MEANING: Record of day-to-day activities; tree trunk

SENTENCE: Lawyers who bill by the hour have to be sure to log all the time they spend on every client's case.

Loquacious: MEANING: Talkative, wordy.

SENTENCE: MIguel is very loquacious and can speak on the telephone for hours.

Lucid: MEANING: Easily understood; clear; intelligible.

SENTENCE: Example sentences are another lucid way of learning vocabulary.

Lull: MEANING: Cause to fall asleep; quieten down

SENTENCE: The continuous reading of vocabulary lulled Miriam to sleep.

Luminous: MEANING: Giving off soft light; shining

SENTENCE: Her happy face was luminous in the twilight.

- M -

Magnanimity: MEANING: Generosity of spirit; unselfishness

SENTENCE: Both sides will have to show magnanimity to reach a compromise.

Maladroit: MEANING: Not skilful; awkward; bungling

SENTENCE: A maladroit movement of his hands caused the car to swerve.

Malfeasance: MEANING: Wrongdoing by a public official

SENTENCE: The high-ranking official's malfeasance was discovered only after he had fled the country.

Malingerer: MEANING: Someone who shirks duty, work or effort, often pretending to be unwell

SENTENCE: The doctor said my son was a malingerer.

Malleable: MEANING: Easily influenced; pliable

SENTENCE: The fans of the governor are as malleable and easily led as sheep.

Maverick: MEANING: Rebel, nonconformist

SENTENCE: Most cop movies feature heroes that are maverick police officers, breaking all the rules, blowing things up, and getting their guns confiscated by the chief – but ultimately saving the day.

Mawkish: MEANING: Effusively or insincerely emotional; excessively sentimental

SENTENCE: The Valentine's Day cards were a bit mawkish to my taste.

Mellifluous: MEANING: Pleasing to the ear

SENTENCE: Ali woke up early to the mellifluous singing of sparrows.

Mendacious: MEANING: Not telling the truth; lying.

SENTENCE: The political party workers had been mendacious throughout the court investigation and as a result they were punished severely.

Mendacity: MEANING: The tendency to be untruthful

SENTENCE: You need to overcome this deplorable mendacity, or no one will ever believe anything you say.

Metamorphosis: MEANING: Change of form or shape.

SENTENCE: The metamorphosis of caterpillar to butterfly is typical of many such changes in animal life.

Meticulous: MEANING: Extremely careful and precise

SENTENCE: She was meticulous in her proofreading and copy-editing business.

Mimicking: MEANING: Copying, imitating

SENTENCE: When Richard was caught mimicking his teacher in a rude way, he was put on detention.

Misanthrope: MEANING: A person who dislikes humankind and avoids human society.

SENTENCE: Hostile and untrusting people can be described as misanthropic.

Mitigate: MEANING: Lessen the extent of a harmful or negative outcome

SENTENCE: Sunscreen is used to mitigate the effects of sun on your skin.

Modicum: MEANING: A small or moderate amount

SENTENCE: When you awarded the Fulbright Scholarship, you will have only a modicum expense of the visa to bear; all major expenses are covered by the scholarship.

Mollify: MEANING: Calm or soothe; gain the good will of

SENTENCE: We tried to mollify the hysterical child by promising her many gifts.

Morbid: MEANING: Suggesting the horror of death and decay

SENTENCE: The stories of the war were morbid and upsetting to the children.

Morose: MEANING: Extremely gloomy and depressed

SENTENCE: She was morose after her aunt passed away.

Mundane: MEANING: Common, ordinary

SENTENCE: He was concerned only with mundane matters; where to park the car, what butcher was best etc.

- N -

Nascent: MEANING: The birth or beginning of something

SENTENCE: If we could identify these revolutionary movements in their nascent state, we would be able to eliminate serious trouble in later years.

Negate: MEANING: Make ineffective by counterbalancing the effect of

SENTENCE: The discovery of one dinosaur jaw negated the wisdom that all dinosaurs were vegetarian; that jaw was from a carnivore.

Nuance: MEANING: Shade of subtle difference in meaning, colour or feeling;

SENTENCE: The unskilled eye of the layperson has difficulty in discerning the nuances of colour in the painting.

- O -

Obdurate: MEANING: Stubborn

SENTENCE: I argued this point with him, but he was obdurate despite all the convincing reasons I could give.

Objurgation: MEANING: Harsh criticism

SENTENCE: When someone receives a severe scolding, they experience objurgation.

Neophyte: MEANING: A person who is brand new to a subject or activity

SENTENCE: Four-day cooking classes are offered to both neophytes and experts.

Nettlesome: MEANING: Causing irritation or annoyance; easily annoyed

SENTENCE: She found the paperwork in her job very nettlesome.

Notoriety: MEANING: Famous but for negative reasons

SENTENCE: The notoriety of Pakistan as a corrupt state is due to its lack of a genuine system for accountability.

Obsequious: MEANING: Servile, fawning

SENTENCE: The famous singer had an entourage of friends and staff, many of whom were obsequious.

Obviate: MEANING: Eliminate a need or difficulty

SENTENCE: To obviate an ant infestation we clean our kitchen regularly.

Occlude: MEANING: Close up, or obstruct (an opening)

SENTENCE: Foundation make-up occludes the pores of our skin.

Officious: MEANING: Excessively eager in giving unwanted advice, interfering

SENTENCE: My colleague can be officious in telling me how to do my job. It is annoying!

Omniscience: MEANING: All-knowing; having infinite knowledge

SENTENCE: Nobody except God can claim to have omniscience.

Onerous: MEANING: Involving a great deal of effort, trouble, or difficulty

SENTENCE: He found his duties increasingly onerous.

Opprobrium: MEANING: A state of extreme dishonour

SENTENCE: He threw a can of drink off the balcony, and earnt opprobrium.

Orthodox: MEANING: Traditional; adhering to what is commonly accepted

SENTENCE: He was an orthodox vegetarian; he did not even eat fish.

Ostentatious: MEANING: Characterized by a pretentious or showy display; designed to impress

SENTENCE: Her dress was a simple design – glamorous without being ostentatious.

- P -

Paradigm: MEANING: Standard example; accepted perspective

SENTENCE: Far from being atypically bawdy, this limerick is a paradigm of the form – nearly all of them rely on off-colour jokes.

Paragon: MEANING: A person or thing regarded as a perfect example of a particular quality.

SENTENCE: My mother was the paragon of kindness; she was beloved by many.

Partisan: MEANING: One-sided; prejudiced

SENTENCE: Our judicial system consists of partisan judges; in order to be promoted as a judge, one should have a strong relationship with a strong political party.

Pathological: MEANING: Caused by physical or mental disease

SENTENCE: Her friend turned out to be a pathological liar, nothing she ever said was true.

Patronising: MEANING: Treating others with condescension

SENTENCE: Experts in a field sometimes appear to patronise people who are less knowledgeable on the subject.

Paucity: MEANING: The presence of something in only small or insufficient quantities

SENTENCE: A paucity of good cheer at the party led to the host turning up the music.

Pedantic: MEANING: Excessively concerned with minor details or rules; overly scrupulous

SENTENCE: His analyses are careful and even painstaking, but never pedantic.

Pedestrian: MEANING: Ordinary; dull

SENTENCE: Vocabulary class without example sentences looks to be pedestrian for many students.

Penchant: MEANING: Liking, preference or strong inclination

SENTENCE: He had a strong penchant for sculpture and owned so many statues.

Perfidious: MEANING: Untrustworthy and deceitful

SENTENCE: The lawyer decided not to represent his perfidious client.

Perfunctory: MEANING: Done routinely and with little interest or care

SENTENCE: Her boyfriend gave her a perfunctory kiss on his way out the door.

Peripheral: MEANING: Not of primary importance

SENTENCE: My main goal is to get into a good graduate school; whether it has good fitness facilities is really a peripheral concern.

Permeable: MEANING: Allowing liquids or gases to pass through

SENTENCE: A frog's skin is permeable to water.

Perspicacious: MEANING: Shrewd, wise, discerning

SENTENCE: For a five-year-old kid, Toby was very perspicacious.

Penury: MEANING: Extreme poverty

SENTENCE: A job loss and family breakdown can lead to penury.

Perennial: MEANING: Lasting for an infinite time; enduring or continually recurring

SENTENCE: His parents had a perennial distrust of the media.

Pervasive: MEANING: Spreading or spread throughout, everywhere

SENTENCE: Talking about the weather is pervasive among adults.

Phlegmatic: MEANING: Having an unemotional and stolidly calm disposition.

SENTENCE: The British character can be phlegmatic compared with the emotional Spanish.

Phony: MEANING: Fake; insincere

SENTENCE: She's such a phony person, pretending to befriend people and then talking about them behind their backs.

Piety: MEANING: Devotion to God or to religious practices.

SENTENCE: The nuns live lives of piety and charitable works.

Placate: MEANING: Pacify; bring peace to

SENTENCE: The teacher tried to placate the upset mother whose child had failed in the class.

Placid: MEANING: Peaceful, calm

SENTENCE: Her dog was quite placid, and did not struggle when the vet gave him an injection.

Plasticity: MEANING: The quality of being easily shaped or moulded

SENTENCE: Fine clay, at the right degree of plasticity, is more useful.

Plethora: MEANING: An abundance or excess or something

SENTENCE: She had a plethora of potential dates; 10 boys asked her out.

Plummet: MEANING: Drop sharply; fall straight down.

SENTENCE: During the first minute or so of a skydive, the diver plummets towards earth in free fall; then, he activates a parachute and floats down at what seems like a relatively leisurely pace.

Polemical: MEANING: Involving controversy or dispute

SENTENCE: Don't discuss politics with your parents; it will only end up in a polemical argument.

Porous: MEANING: Full of holes or openings

SENTENCE: The border between the USA and Mexico was porous before they built the wall.

Pragmatic: MEANING: A person or solution that takes a realistic approach

SENTENCE: My daughter wants a unicorn for her birthday, which isn't very pragmatic.

Platitude: MEANING: A trite or obvious remark; a cliche

SENTENCE: The pep talk the boss gave to his team was full of platitudes.

Preamble: MEANING: Introductory statement, preface

SENTENCE: His early publications were just a preamble to his later, extensive written works.

Preclude: MEANING: Prevent from happening, make impossible

SENTENCE: Taking the Pill precluded her from falling pregnant.

Precariously: MEANING: Dangerously

SENTENCE: The glass was precariously balanced on the edge of the table.

Precipitate: MEANING: cause something to happen suddenly, unexpectedly and not always in a good way

SENTENCE: The assassination of the Archbishop precipitated World War Two.

Prevarication: MEANING: The deliberate act of deviating from the truth

SENTENCE: The reporter said that he is extremely sorry for spreading the prevarications about the Prime Minister's death in the hospital.

Pristine: MEANING: Unspoiled; remaining in a pure state

SENTENCE: Much of the coastline of Australia is made up of pristine beaches.

Precursor: MEANING: Something that comes before, and indicates that something will follow

SENTENCE: Pride is a precursor to a fall.

Probity: MEANING: The quality of having strong moral principles; honesty and decency

SENTENCE: She showed great probity in the divorce process and they split amicably.

Prescient: MEANING: Having or showing knowledge of events before they take place

SENTENCE: It is difficult, now, to appreciate just how prescient her art work was.

Problematic: MEANING: Constituting or presenting a problem.

SENTENCE: The COVID-19 lockdown was problematic for businesses and employees.

Presumptuous: MEANING: Taking liberties, bold forwardness

SENTENCE: I hope I won't be considered presumptuous if I offer you some advice.

Prodigal: MEANING: Rashly or wastefully extravagant

SENTENCE: Out of all the family, their uncle was the most prodigal, and they bailed him out frequently.

Profound: MEANING: Very insightful; deep

SENTENCE: She realised the book offered some very profound messages on our current society.

Prevaricate: MEANING: Be deliberately ambiguous in order to mislead

SENTENCE: His style was to prevaricate, but she saw through him and got to the truth.

Prohibitive: MEANING: Tending to discourage (especially prices)

SENTENCE: The books were made browser-proof with prohibitive cellophane wrapping.

Proliferate: MEANING: Increase rapidly in number; multiply

SENTENCE: Science fiction magazines proliferated in the 1920s.

Prolific: MEANING: Productive; fruitful

SENTENCE: She wrote three songs before breakfast; she was a prolific songwriter in this stage of her career.

Propensity: MEANING: An inclination or natural tendency to behave in a particular way

SENTENCE: The dog has a propensity to bark, and we have a propensity to be annoyed by it!

Proscribe: MEANING: Forbid, especially by law

SENTENCE: The headmaster proscribed the use of mobile phones in the classroom.

Protracted: MEANING: Drawn out for a long time, in a tedious way

SENTENCE: The protracted heat had the effect of driving people away from the city yesterday.

Prudent: MEANING: Wise; judicious.

SENTENCE: Her partner was prudent with their money and their future, which made her very happy!

Punctiliously: MEANING: Fastidiously, very carefully

SENTENCE: British soldiers act punctiliously at the changing of the guard at Buckingham Palace.

Propitiate: MEANING: win or regain favour; appease

SENTENCE: He propitiated his mother on Mother's Day with a bouquet and a box of chocolates.

Pungent: MEANING: Having a sharply strong taste or smell

SENTENCE: This homegrown garlic has a particularly pungent flavour.

Propriety: MEANING: Conforming to good manners or appropriate behaviour

SENTENCE: They questioned the propriety of certain investments made by the council.

- Q -

Qualified: MEANING: officially recognized as being trained to perform a particular job; certified

SENTENCE: I was well qualified with a degree to teach the class English vocabulary!

Quibble: MEANING: Small fight or argument over something unimportant

SENTENCE: She did not want to quibble over a few euros when she bought the dog from the pet shop.

Quiescent: MEANING: Resting, quiet

SENTENCE: He enjoyed quiescent moments in his garden hammock on a beautiful summer Sunday.

Quotidian: MEANING: Daily, routine, ordinary

SENTENCE: She enjoyed all things quotidian: doing chores, brushing her teeth, going to work, because she had a happy nature.

- R -

Rankle: MEANING: Aggravate; make angry

SENTENCE: We did not want to rankle the cat, so we put the puppy outside.

Rarefied: MEANING: Elevated above the ordinary

SENTENCE: The scholars were in an animated and rarefied conversation about world politics.

Rebuttal: MEANING: A counter argument to argument; a disagreement

SENTENCE: Steve rebutted Jason's view that his team would win the game.

Recalcitrant: MEANING: Obstinately uncooperative; pig-headed

SENTENCE: She has a class of recalcitrant fifteen-year-olds.

Recant: MEANING: Take back something that was previously said

SENTENCE: Heretics were burned if they did not recant.

Recluse: MEANING: A person who lives a solitary life and tends to avoid other people

SENTENCE: After returning from the pilgrimage she has turned into a virtual recluse.

Recondite: MEANING: Difficult to comprehend; abstruse

SENTENCE: The book on mathematical theory is full of recondite information.

Refractory: MEANING: Stubborn or unmanageable

SENTENCE: My dog is refractory on the lead; he does not want to walk!

Refute: MEANING: Prove to be false

SENTENCE: She refuted her kids' claim they had brushed their teeth by producing the dry toothbrushes.

Relegate: MEANING: Assign to an inferior rank or position

SENTENCE: Their soccer team was relegated to third division in the new season.

Reproach: MEANING: Criticize.

SENTENCE: I want my work to be above reproach and without error

Reprobate: MEANING: An unprincipled person; a bad egg

SENTENCE: The politician had to present himself as more of a lovable reprobate than a purely corrupt official.

Repudiate: MEANING: Refuse to accept; reject.

SENTENCE: As an adult, Ben repudiated the religion of his upbringing and went to work on Sundays.

Rescind: MEANING: Revoke, cancel, or repeal (a law, order, or agreement)

SENTENCE: The government eventually rescinded the policy after it faced severe criticism from both the opposition and the public.

Resolution: MEANING: Quality of being firmly determined

SENTENCE: Given the many areas of conflict still awaiting resolution, the outcome of the peace talks remains problematic.

Resolve: MEANING: Settle or find a solution to a problem or contentious matter

SENTENCE: The firm aims to resolve problems within 30 days

Reticent: MEANING: Quiet, restrained

SENTENCE: She was reticent about her feelings in his company as she did not know him very well.

Revelling: MEANING: Taking great pleasure

SENTENCE: After receiving the job offer she revelled all weekend with her family and friends.

Reverent: MEANING: Feeling or showing deep and solemn respect

SENTENCE: In church there is a reverent silence when the priest says, 'Let us pray.'

Rudimentary: MEANING: Basic; crude

SENTENCE: The test will be easy; it only requires a rudimentary knowledge of English.

- S -

Sagacious: MEANING: Acutely wise, very shrewd

SENTENCE: The president acquired some sagacious advisors to help him with managing the economy.

Sage: MEANING: A profoundly wise man, especially in ancient history or legend

SENTENCE: Aristotle, the great Athenian philosopher, was undoubtedly a sage.

Salubrious: MEANING: Conducive to health or wellbeing

SENTENCE: After spending many years smoking and drinking, Tom recognized the necessity of adopting a more salubrious lifestyle.

Sanction: MEANING: Approve, give permission; punish, speak harshly to

SENTENCE: America's sanctions on Cuba mean that it is illegal for Americans to do business with Cuban companies.

Sanguine: MEANING: Confidently optimistic and cheerful

SENTENCE: The whole family was sanguine about their chances of going on holiday.

Satiate: MEANING: Satisfy

SENTENCE: The Japanese meal did not satiate him and he ate a sandwich when he got home.

Saturate: MEANING: Soak thoroughly

SENTENCE: The rain saturated the field and caused the river to rise.

Saturnine: MEANING: Gloomy, mean, scowling

SENTENCE: Do not be misled by his saturnine appearance; he is not as gloomy as he looks.

Savour: MEANING: Appreciate fully; taste something savoury

SENTENCE: As a parent, it's important to take a step back and really savour the special moments –those children will grow up sooner than you think.

Scathing: MEANING: Very harsh or severe

SENTENCE: Joseph suffered scathing criticism from the judge at the singing competition.

Scrupulous: MEANING: Careful to do things properly or correctly

SENTENCE: She was scrupulous with repaying her friends straight away if they lent her money.

Secrete: MEANING: Conceal, hide; release

SENTENCE: HIs assets had been secreted to Swiss bank accounts

Shard: MEANING: A broken piece of a brittle artifact

SENTENCE: Shards of glass flew in all directions

Skeptic: MEANING: One who doubts others unless they have seen evidence

SENTENCE: She was sceptical about her sister's claim she had seen a ghost!

Solicitous: MEANING: Full of anxiety and concern; showing hovering attentiveness

SENTENCE: She was tiny and solicitous, a soft, sweet lady.

Soporific: MEANING: Tending to induce drowsiness or sleep

SENTENCE: The motion of the train had a somewhat soporific effect.

Spartan: MEANING: Practicing great self-denial, unsparing and uncompromising in discipline or judgement

SENTENCE: Her apartment was so spartan that she couldn't even serve us both soups; she only had one bowl and one spoon.

Spasmodically: MEANING: In spurts and fits; with spasms

SENTENCE: The newborn giraffe lies in a sodden heap, heaving spasmodically with its first gulps of air.

Specious: MEANING: Plausible but false; deceptively pleasing

SENTENCE: Misinformation, falsehoods and specious claims dominate his public pronouncements.

Sporadic: MEANING: Recurring in scattered and irregular or unpredictable instances

SENTENCE: In the last few decades, the west has been subjected to sporadic terrorist bombings.

Stigma: MEANING: A negative association

SENTENCE: These days there is far less stigma attached to being in a same sex relationship.

Stingy: MEANING: Not generous with money

SENTENCE: Many companies are too stingy to raise the salaries of their workers.

Stint: MEANING: Be very economical about spending; an unbroken period of time

SENTENCE: He doesn't stint on wining and dining – every night he spends hundreds of dollars in restaurants and bars

Stipulate: MEANING: Specify as a condition or requirement in a contract or agreement

SENTENCE: He stipulated certain conditions before their marriage

Stolid: MEANING: Showing little emotion; expressionless

SENTENCE: Her face was stolid, but inside she was thrilled.

Substantiate: MEANING: Give support to a claim

SENTENCE: More evidence of the Tooth Fairy is needed to substantiate her existence.

Superficiality: MEANING: Lack of depth of knowledge or thought or feeling; shallowness

SENTENCE: Instant digital interactions, on your phone or computer, encourage superficiality, insularity and tribalism.

Strife: MEANING: State of fighting or arguing violently

SENTENCE: Strife in the Middle East has continued for many, many years.

Supersede: MEANING: Take the place or move into the position of

SENTENCE: When his father passed away, Toby superseded him as head of the family.

Strut: MEANING: Walk with a proud swagger with a little arrogance thrown in

SENTENCE: After hitting his third six, the batsman strutted down the pitch.

Subpoena: MEANING: A writ ordering a person to attend a court

SENTENCE: The courier delivered the subpoena to her door and she had to sign for it.

Subside: MEANING: Wear off or die down; sink to a lower level; descend

SENTENCE: The world waited patiently for the danger of COVID-19 to subside.

Supposition: MEANING: An assumption or hypothesis

SENTENCE: They were working on the supposition that his death was murder.

Sycophant: MEANING: A person who tries to win favour from powerful people by flattering them

SENTENCE: The fans backstage we very sycophantic.

- T -

Tacit: MEANING: Understood, without actually being expressed; implied

SENTENCE: They were holding hands; it was tacit they were lovers.

Taciturn: MEANING: Talking little, reserved

SENTENCE: Desmond's taciturn behaviour in front of the Fulbright decision panel has made his interview awkward, hence the panel has rejected him for the scholarship.

Tangential: MEANING: Of superficial relevance, if any

SENTENCE: She made some tangential remarks on her sister's career, and then changed the subject.

Thrift: MEANING: Great care in spending money

SENTENCE: In older age, most people become thrifty and tend to save money as much as possible.

Timorous: MEANING: Timid, shy

SENTENCE: In big groups she was timorous, but with close friends she was very outgoing.

Tirade: MEANING: Long string of violent, emotionally charged words

SENTENCE: There are many tirades in the speeches of politicians in parliament.

Temperance: MEANING: Moderation, restraint

SENTENCE: Noted for his temperance, he seldom drinks alcohol.

Torpor: MEANING: Mental and physical inactivity

SENTENCE: After the huge meal at the fiesta, the family fell into a torpor and did not manage to dance.

Tenuous: MEANING: Very thin or slight

SENTENCE: There is a tenuous link between interest rates and investment.

Torrid: MEANING: Very hot; passionate and emotionally charged

SENTENCE: It was the most torrid romance she had ever been lucky enough to find.

Tortuous: MEANING: Full of twists and turns

SENTENCE: The route to Cairns from Brisbane in Australia is remote and tortuous.

Tractable: MEANING: Easily managed or controlled

SENTENCE: Emerging sequencing technologies can provide extra information and make the computational problem more tractable.

Transgression: MEANING: An act that goes against a law, rule, or code of conduct; an offense.

SENTENCE: I'll be keeping an eye out for further transgressions from that employee.

Trifling: MEANING: Unimportant

SENTENCE: After he interrupted the teacher with some trifling matter, the teacher resumed the class.

Truculence: MEANING: Obstreperous and defiant aggression

SENTENCE: The basketball team won through sheer truculence; there were lots of fouls in the game.

Tumultuous: MEANING: Troubled and disordered, turbulent

SENTENCE: The police presence ensured there was not a tumultuous reaction to the extension of lockdown.

- U -

Ubiquitous: MEANING: Existing everywhere at the same time

SENTENCE: Facebook, Coca-Cola and Hollywood are ubiquitous American inventions.

Umbrage: MEANING: A feeling of anger caused by being offended

SENTENCE: I took umbrage at the suggestion that I was lazy, as I work eight hours a day.

Underscore: MEANING: To emphasize, call special attention to

SENTENCE: He underscored his points in the debate.

Unseemly: MEANING: Indecent; inappropriate; unacceptable

SENTENCE: Heather's uncle made unseemly suggestions to her friend when they were alone.

- V -

Vacillation: MEANING: Moving back and forth; changing of opinion

SENTENCE: There was a fair bit of vacillation on Steven's part, he could not make up his mind.

Venerate: MEANING: Worship, adore, be in awe of

SENTENCE: You probably don't venerate your teacher or your boss, however you may act like you do!

Veracious: MEANING: Truthful; precisely accurate

SENTENCE: While we elect our leaders in the hope that everything that they say will be veracious, history has shown that such a hope is naive.

Verbose: MEANING: Using or containing too many words

SENTENCE: This article is too verbose; nobody has enough time to read the whole article, so we must edit it to make it brief and to the point.

Viable: MEANING: Able to function properly, able to grow

SENTENCE: The infant, though prematurely born, is viable and has a good chance of survival.

Vindicate: MEANING: Show to be right by providing justification or proof; clear of blame; defend

SENTENCE: The governor's policy on lockdown was vindicated by the drop in coronavirus deaths; his decision to extend it was the right one.

Viscous: MEANING: Having a thick, sticky consistency between solid and liquid; having a high viscosity.

SENTENCE: It seemed to take forever for the viscous cough medicine to pour out of the bottle.

Vituperative: MEANING: Marked by harshly abusive criticism; scathing

SENTENCE: Scots who opposed independence hurled vituperative insults at the independence party.

Vociferous: MEANING: Offensively loud; given to vehement outcry

SENTENCE: Some states in the US are contending with vociferous protests as they extend lockdown for COVID-19.

Volatile: MEANING: Liable to lead to sudden change; tending to vary often

SENTENCE: Sophie's relationship with Dave can be volatile; they fight and make up regularly.

Volubility: MEANING: The quality of being effortless in speech and writing

SENTENCE: The volubility in his expression shows his level of knowledge in the topic.

- W -

Warranted: MEANING: Justified or shown to be reasonable; provide adequate ground for

SENTENCE: The employees feel that industrial action is warranted

Wary: MEANING: Very cautious; on guard

SENTENCE: Be wary of anyone who tells you that 'anyone' can get rich with some special plan or scheme.

Welter: MEANING: Move in a turbulent fashion; a confused multitude of things; be immersed in

SENTENCE: Easter was solemnly marked amid the welter of death and suffering due to COVID-19.

Whimsical: MEANING: Determined by chance or whim; indulging in or influenced by fancy

SENTENCE: The plot and characters in *Peter Pan* are quite whimsical.

- Z -

Zeal: MEANING: Eager enthusiasm; prompt willingness; excessive fervour.

SENTENCE: Each inherited their parents' zeal for social justice.

BLANK NOTES SECTION

....
....
....
....
....
....
....
....
....
....
....
....
....
....
....
....
....

....

....

....

....

....

....

....

....

....

....

....

....

....

....

....

....

....

....

....

....

....

....

....

....

....

....

....

....

....

....

....

....

....

....

....

....

....

....

....

....

....

....

....

....

....

....

....

....

....

....

....

....

....

FREE ONLINE ENGLISH RESOURCES FOR IELTS

This is a great video activity site with clips and questions around films and TV series. It has different levels and is great for listening and speaking skills (pronunciation).

https://www.eslvideo.com/

Online Pronunciation Dictionary by Cambridge University.

https://dictionary.cambridge.org/browse/pronunciation/english/

THANK YOU

I hope you've found it useful!

As I mentioned in the foreword, a lot of hard work has gone into this project.

My whole objective with this book is to help you reach your ultimate goal of achieving an 8.5 in your IELTS test. This book is not designed to be an exhaustive list of words, but instead, a focused and easy-access guide for exam preparation. Review any sections that you feel you need to and use them as a starting point for further research and practice.

What Now?

In the next few pages, you'll find a massive bundle of free resources you can get hold of, including letter and email templates, presentation templates and grammar and vocabulary resource books! As a free member with exclusive access to my free starter library, you'll also get free reports, books and articles to help you take your English to the next level!

If you enjoyed this book, I'd be very grateful if you'd post a short review on Amazon. Your support really does make a difference and means a lot to me. I read all the reviews personally, so I can get your feedback and make this book even better in the future.

Thanks for your support.

MEGA-BONUS: MARC ROCHE'S ENTIRE STARTER LIBRARY OF FREE BOOKS!

Sign up to the free VIP List today, to grab your downloadable e-books ☺

I hope you have found this book useful. Thank you for reading.

https://www.idmadrid.es/vip-resources

Bonus Chapter: FREE BOOK! The Productivity Cheat Sheet

Download your free copy of The Productivity Cheat Sheet: 15 Secrets of Productivity here!

https://www.idmadrid.es/vip-resources

Printed in Great Britain
by Amazon

85718020R20150